T0195552

A
LIFE
ALTERING
SCAR

HOW FAMILY, FAITH, AND LAUGHTER HELPED

JUNE LaROSE

authorHOUSE'

AuthorHouse™
1663 Liberty Drive
Bloomington, IN 47403
www.authorhouse.com
Phone: 1 (800) 839-8640

Published by AuthorHouse 02/28/2020

ISBN: 978-1-7283-4874-2 (sc)
ISBN: 978-1-7283-4875-9 (e)

"The beautiful part of writing is that you don't have to get it right the first time. You can revise and rewrite until you are satisfied. Unlike brain surgery."

Author Unknown

INTRODUCTION

All of us have or will have struggles in our lives that end up causing scars we could never imagine we would accumulate. I am no exception. In fact, I have earned many altering marks in my lifetime. This story is how I handled, a **larger-than-life,** altering scar I obtained when I found out I had a brain tumor and needed a craniotomy.

Since I did not want this to devastate me, I needed to find a way to turn it into something constructive. Fully aware this would be problematic at best and perhaps even fatal, I felt compelled to capture it, then write about the experience. That desire became a quest for knowledge, so I could share it knowing this could help others. This story is all true with one exception. The names of individuals in this memoir, (that are not my family) have been changed.

With personal experience being my teacher, I learned what it felt like to be on the other side of unyielding insanity, and my family had to learn how to deal with that person. Some of the situations we went through were extremely terrifying and emotionally painful. Some of the episodes for me included: horrifying hallucinations, looming death, and all the resulting turmoil the family had to deal with. Relearning how to talk, walk, and find my new normal became my challenges. Much of what transpired was a struggle, **yet** parts of it were truly remarkable.

CONTENTS

1   What the Hell Just Happened? 1

2   The Reflection in the Mirror! 5

3   Voices Threw Me Over the Edge 10

4   The Mystery is Partially Revealed 14

5   The Full Reveal 19

6   Reminiscing Turns into Mental Gymnastics 23

7   In an Emotional Washing Machine 28

8   Research Tiptoed in Like a Herd of Elephants 33

9   Signs I Had Ignored 36

10   The Surgery Could NOT be Stopped 41

11   The Light of God 43

12   On the "Trip" to Recovery 46

13   Drainage Tube is Removed 51

14   Brain Dead 54

15   Russell's Turn to Experience the Nightmare 62

16   I Tried to be Strong 69

17   The "Fight" to Go Home 72

18   Lack of Physical Coordination 76

19   The Adventure of Recovery 78

20   A New "Me" 83

21   New Hairstyle Brings Emotional Wellness 86

22   I Never Gave Up 88

Acknowledgements and Gratitude 91

Appendix A—Pictures 93

Works Cited 97

1

What the Hell Just Happened?

Life being what it is and never perfect, I had been laid off in the fall of 2009. Since the world continued recovering from the Great Recession of '08, I was now on a career detour. There I was at the age of 56, needing to make yet another life changing decision. Should I take this opportunity to go back to college, to finish my lifelong dream to attain a degree, then obtain a better occupation or retire from work completely? I found it easier to make the decision when I realized I could use my husband's VA plan to help finance the cost. When I finished (with high honors) in December of 2011, I felt confident it would take no time at all to obtain employment. How wrong I was. Five months later, I still had not heard back from any of the jobs I had applied to. After reviewing my paperwork, I discovered several résumés and cover letters that had gone out, had errors in them. I now lived with shame and humiliation. What would be revealed to me very soon was…my processing ability had been compromised.

Around that same time, my daughter Mindy came to me and her stepfather Roy with tears in her eyes, asking if she and Michael (her 12-year-old son) could move back in with us. Without hesitation we agreed to help them. Michael could be good company for me especially since my husband, worked a lot of hours. Roy is a facility manager plus he volunteers. He is the VFW vice commander at our local post and he volunteers as a ranger two days a week at a golf course.

Roy and Mindy would leave the house early and I would be there for Michael in-between him catching the bus to and from school. It was fun watching him and the boys in the neighborhood as they enjoyed their friendships. I became the stay at home Nana bringing them cookies and treats. A couple of weeks into our new routine everything seemed to be settling down nicely. That is until Michael called out, "Nana, there's some lady on the phone asking to talk with you. She said something about the employment agency." That all-essential call I had been waiting for had arrived. They called to let me know I had been hired at a phone company. I just needed to fill out paperwork so I could start work on Monday. Finally, we will be back on track. I will pick up the medical insurance and Roy would finally be able to retire.

Thursday, June 7, 2012, the very next day, after everyone returned to work and school. Bizarre events began to occur causing me to realize life really does have more dimensions than I ever imagined possible. In a flash, my once familiar world was no longer real. As I stood by the kitchen island an unexpected sense of dread engulfed my whole body. My kitchen became obscured and unfamiliar. While attempting to clear the fog in my head an extremely urgent pressure to vomit arose. Now struggling to prevent having this all over my floor, I needed to rush towards the powder room. Although the room is only three steps away, I still had that automatic reaction to slap my mouth closed. With my mind now whirling, *I am not going to make it,* the spew exploded into the porcelain bowl. With one very large heave it was out. It was obvious to me that was no ordinary vomit. It was a violent projectile. This happened so quickly it left me with no time to even think, yet one thought emerged crystal clear, *I'm not even sick, what fresh misery was that?*

Still very confused, the possible causes kept swimming in my head, but they were more to excuse the behavior away than to comprehend it. *Maybe an extreme sinus infection or food poisoning?* Yet, none of that made any sense nor mattered, because what happened next threw me into agonizing pain and terrifying fear.

With extreme fatigue pushing me, my disoriented focus was now trying to steer me in the correct direction to our couch. Even though it stood less than eight steps away, I found it exceptionally hard to reach. When I laid down, the exhaustion was so abrupt it left me feeling pinned to the couch. As I lay there an invisible force began beating me in the face with two steel beams. The intensity was so vivid I actually visualized them smashing onto my face. Each beam was ½ inch thick, twice as wide and approximately eight inches long. They were using my face like a drum, pounding in a rhythmic fashion as though trying to summon troops to war. The beams were suspended in midair maneuvering without help. With every connection they sent excruciating pain echoing throughout my whole body. My cheek, taking the brunt of the force, felt as though it was fracturing with every connection. My heart began racing with fear while my disjointed mind kept trying to speculate why the beams were slamming on my face. Yet, I was too drained to even think because another blow is thrust upon my cheekbone. All I could do was wrench in pain. Haphazardly, my battered thoughts suggested, ***bring your hands up, let them take the blunt of the hit***. But I couldn't, not a single part of me could move. My whole body appeared to be shackled by heavy weights. My mind screamed out, **"*WHY ARE YOU BEATING ON ME?*"** Feeling helpless as another blow smashed my face, I pleaded and screamed out, ***SSTTTOOPPP!!***

Instantly the atmosphere changed. The whole room became saturated with soft classical music. In a flash the room washed with calmness. I felt my rigid body soften as everything became peaceful and the beating stopped. I remember thinking it feels like angels have come to play exclusively to soothe the invisible beast away from me. The pain vanished and I distinctly remember feeling a small smile form upon my lips and eyes. As I drifted off to sleep, every part of what just took place vanished from my short-term memory. Beyond that nothing. My rational mind shut down due to the damage. That incident was now registered null and void as I blanked out. My brain just excused everything away and tucked it into a secret file in my mind.

For the next two days, a lot of what took place was void of time for me. The rest of Thursday, Friday, and part of Saturday morning, I functioned with no memory of my actions or previous occurrences. That is, except for the fact that I had slept on the couch those two days due to exhaustion.

2

The Reflection in the Mirror!

On Saturday morning, I finally managed to pull myself somewhat together. Armed with no memory of the past few days, I nonchalantly went upstairs for a much-needed shower and change of clothes. Mindy was at work; Roy was relaxing in the family room reading the newspaper while Michael enjoyed cartoons.

Grabbing some clean clothes out of the closet, I headed towards the master bath. As I reached the doorway, the nearby surroundings instantly melted away when I saw an obscure entity in the mirror. As I attempted to focus in better, my eyes automatically kept opening wider and wider as my heart began to race and my body trembled in fear. The image had me thinking I was viewing it in 3D as though I could reach out and touch it. My mind started struggling to right this abnormality. That caused my brainwaves to feel scrunched up and confused, as a part of me semi-realized I couldn't possibly be seeing that correctly. A very wrinkled apparition with long gray hair stood trapped in the bathroom mirror. The haggard woman wrapped in gray rags stood there staring mindlessly. She was standing upright framed by a wooden entranceway in the shape of a coffin. The gray smoke that engulfed the image made the surroundings appear to be floating towards me. Totally petrified, I was unable to even swallow. My concentration became completely locked on the image. The sad loneliness in her eyes and on her face, brought me to one undisputed conclusion, someone or thing had abused her. It wasn't visual bruising; it was the kind of abuse that steals your soul and ambition to live.

Although I desperately wanted to flee, I couldn't move a single muscle. It felt as though I was being challenged to figure out what it truly was. Struggling to engage the correct brain connections, the apparition gradually moved out of the mirror as my image finally came into focus. Yet… "that new image" pushed me even deeper into shock as reality gave me "my" persona; I was now filled with more questions than answers.

What I saw now was…I am the one who is marked with bruises, cuts, and swelling. Dreadfully wanting to divorce all of this from my sense of being, I questioned out loud, "Why am I so swollen and marked up? And, why hasn't anyone else in the house noticed and told me how I look?" Utterly disoriented, it became essential to walk away, as the reality of this was extremely harsh to accept. While walking away, I kept instinctively shaking my head NO, not wanting any of this to be real.

Utterly stunned, I reluctantly proceeded to examine my body to see if I could confirm what was or wasn't real. Adding to my confusion, the injuries only appeared on the left side of my body. Deep purple, blue, and green marks were on my cheek, chin, and down my arm. Along with scrapes and cuts on my elbow and my forearm. A large bluish-green bruise the size of a large grapefruit appeared on my upper deltoid muscle. It seemed like I had been used as a punching bag, yet none of it hurt. And, I had no idea **how** I got that way! Totally overwhelmed with more questions than answers my first rational questions were: *Who the hell beat me up? Why don't I feel pain or know WHAT happened to me?* My emotions were falling all over the place. I appeared to be in someone else's body, and "I" no longer existed!

Out of angry frustration I asked myself again, *Why hasn't anyone else noticed this? How could no one else in the house **not see** all these bruises, scrapes, and swelling? They do see me, don't they?*

My emotions were frustrated and stunned. That pushed the core of my existence to an extremely sad empty place. My whole being acknowledged, it was now imperative to know what was real. It became essential to validate all of this with someone else. Filled with anxious anticipation, I found my way back to the family room where Roy was reading.

That apparition, the one that first appeared in the mirror, became another forgotten memory. Not a word was mentioned to anyone about it. Although not obvious to me, my mind must have been running on one track at a time. The focus moved to the marks on me and how they got there. I asked Roy quite casually, "Does my face look swollen to you?" He moved the newspaper down so he could look at me. With a raised eyebrow, and a sense of apprehension that I even asked, he examined my face. His probing looks quickly turned to disbelief.

"You look like shit! What did you do?" With sheer sadness I thought, *That validated what I saw, but you could have been more sympathetic.* Shaking my head and rolling my eyes, I started to walk away. Immediately realizing what he had just done, in a more apologetic voice he said, "How did you get so bruised and cut up?"

My face contorted into an angry pissed off bitch look, as I was becoming emotionally unraveled. All I could say as I snapped back, "I honestly don't know." And I thought, *You obviously don't care.* With even more irritation in my voice, "I must have bumped into something, but I don't remember how, what, where, or even when it happened."

Michael had been listening intently to our conversation from the living room. Roy then walked into the kitchen to gather his thoughts. But I needed to talk more about it. So, I pushed and questioned harder to find out what had happened. My mind remained on one track, but my emotions tumbled all over the place playing very unkind tricks on me.

The emotion that made sense at this moment was being angry that no one seemed to care, so I ran with it. Those reactions however, changed as we gathered in the kitchen and began to look around the room trying to answer the immediate question, "What really caused those marks?"

As the three of us gathered to look for clues I said, "I must have fallen…how else could I have gotten bruised and scraped so badly? Yet I don't remember that happening." And even though exasperated with the situation only a moment ago, I had quickly become pleased and cheerful.

My thoughts were whirling, *Had I fallen, bump into the wall? Why don't I know what is going on?* The not knowing had me even more anxious than what had occurred. Everything seemed to be disconnected and I began to feel childish. This whole situation brought out a childish happy-go-lucky demeanor within me.

(My mind continuously took over my emotions and I never knew what reaction was coming out next. It is obvious when the mind and the body do not coexist, insanity shows up).

The search now became a game as we gathered to solve the mystery. It felt as though I was playing a children's game. With a rhetorical, juvenile flair I questioned, "Let's say I fell. How could that take place without my knowledge? How could anyone fall, get up, and carry on without realizing it?" The evidence showed something like that took place, so we soldiered on with the search.

"You know," Roy said, (while conjuring up his memory) "The other day I wiped something sticky off the kitchen floor near the cupboards thinking it was ketchup or syrup someone spilled."

Hearing those words brought me to a complete stop as I perked up to listen. My heart raced with anticipation for more clues; I became so excited and giddy knowing that a clue had been exposed. Thoughts began running through my mind, but I was speechless. *Had I fallen there? Was it **my** blood on the floor?* Feeling the full answer might be near, I became enthusiastic and filled with gratitude.

As for Roy, he felt he had **Solved the mystery**! So without another word he went upstairs to shower and start his day.

Completely stunned by his behavior and extremely agitated, my thoughts, eyes, and feelings all bulged out as I wanted to scream. My thoughts rang out, *Whhhyy are you going **upstairs**?! I'm still confused!* But nothing was said out loud. *Damn men. Ssometimes I just wish I could throttle them!*

While going through this, I hadn't a clue I ignored everything. I became so out of touch with reality, my mind would not allow me to come to terms with what was hallucination or reality, or what the appropriate emotion should be. I wanted to cry, but I wasn't sure why. My body, brain, and emotions no longer could distinguish what or how to feel. I was becoming exhausted from all the emotional flipping and flopping. Every part of me was acting as though they were out of their given element and could not grasp how to act or maneuver. I caved in and gave up not knowing how to proceed. It was as though someone had given me a drug or taken over my body and mind remotely. I no longer existed as me and it felt like I had no control to return. Although I never took illicit drugs, my mind definitely appeared to be functioning as though they were a part of this scene as I drifted in and out of reality. The delusional state had not stopped there. In fact, it began to accelerate. It is obvious to me only after my recovery that this, could be happen and had transpired.

3

• • ● ● ● • •

Voices Threw Me Over the Edge

After Roy went upstairs, I went back into the family room to mull over what I had just learned. Standing in the room for a moment, I must have cocooned myself into a flight of fancy, because out of nowhere, voices resonated from the other room. I peered through our interior window, the view which passes through the kitchen into our dining room, attempting to determine what the noise was. No one was in sight, yet the soft voices continued. The voices were low, as though in a private meeting. Looking deeper into the room, I still saw nothing. I found it amusing as I listened and my thoughts drifted, *I am wide awake and definitely not dreaming. Why am I hearing voices, and what are they doing in our dining room? Do **they** know what happened? Is that what they are discussing?* Staring deeper into the room I could now almost visualize them standing off to the right. Forcefully trying to connect the correct neurons to find clarity, my attention kicked into high gear. Well, as high as it could at that time. Instead of clarity, peace engulfed me, leaving me to be filled with awe. I was not worried, frightened, or anxious. It was obvious, even to me, I truly had no control over my thoughts. However, my subconscious was able to make one slightly sane decision. I was not going to tell anyone about the voices because I did <u>not</u> want them to know I was going crazy.

However, the thought that there were more unanswered questions remained. It kept my inner spirit awake and continuously pushing for more clues. The following morning, I awoke with an inner thirst that just would not be quenched until I knew exactly what was occurring. It was as though my subconscious mind kept whispering, *Something isn't right. It is time for **you** to take charge for you.* I wasn't worried or afraid. Only curiosity lived within me.

After breakfast, while sitting in the living room, I started to talk about what might have taken place. I questioned why am I so oblivious about how I obtained the bruises and cuts. Roy put down the Sunday newspaper, and Mindy sat down to talk to me before going to work. Mindy wanted to know, in detail, what my symptoms were. They both asked more questions and were now insisting I see a doctor to find out what had transpired. Roy commented that I was being unrealistic and irrational, as though he was trying to convince **me**. But my inner being was aware there was something wrong. And although that was the extent of the conversation, I finally felt like we had all moved into the same direction.

Suddenly, out of the clear blue, I felt an urgent obligation to bring my son Russell and daughter-in-law Claire, who live in Virginia, into the loop. I sent a picture of myself along with a brief explanation via my cell phone, to let them know what was occurring. Russell agreed I should at least be checked by a doctor, especially since I had not a clue what had happened to me.

All of that pushing helped me to feel better emotionally, although I was clueless to why. Mindy now insisted I go to Urgent Care, where she worked, to be checked out. She said she would pre-register me so I wouldn't have to wait. We all agreed to meet her at Urgent Care later that morning. Since she was their opener, we had to wait for her to get to work. Strangely enough, I still felt everything was going to be just fine.

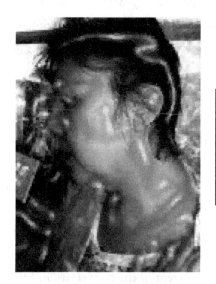

Swelling and
bruising on the
cheek bone and
down my face

Bruising on
Deltoid Muscle

Swelling cuts
and scraps

4

••••••

The Mystery is Partially Revealed

On Sunday, June 10th, none of us could have predicted we were about to travel to the land of the unknown. With a lot of curiosity and little-to-no fear in my heart, Roy, Michael, and I embarked on what we thought would be just a short visit to the doctor's office. When we arrived, the parking lot was already full. Once inside, Roy searched for a place to sit while I went to the front desk to talk to Mindy. Her demeanor was stiff and sharp as I approached the desk. It was obvious to me that she was a little stressed, because she wouldn't even look at me. It felt like she was struggling to stayed poised, when with a tone of anxious authority, she said, "Mom, I was not able to pre-register you. I didn't have time because there were patients waiting at the door when I arrived this morning. But I had time to talk to the doctor and insisted you be seen by Lea, the best physician assistant (PA) we have here." She handed me a clipboard with a form on it. "You need to fill out this paperwork before you can be seen. Let me know when you are done."

That matter-of-fact behavior was so out of character for her. She is usually happy-go-lucky and upbeat. She is the one who tries to keep everyone else in good spirits. I sensed from her unusual demeanor that she found out something about my symptoms that caused her concern. But I was still not worried. When I brought the form back, she said, again in a straightforward tone, "Lea is in with another patient, but as soon as she is finished, you will be called in."

With a slight nod of my head and a smile I told her, "I'm fine, don't worry, everything will be okay." She only half smiled back.

As I went back to sit with Roy, the waiting room became irrelevant as I barely noticed the other patients waiting. What is usually a room thick with uncertainties and several ill patients, was now just an ordinary room with strangers. My concerns were focused on nothing specific, not even my issues, because I was not truly all there.

It wasn't long before Mindy came out to tell us Lea was available. She also insisted, "I am coming in the room with you!"

No interpretation was called for, her decision was conclusive. She was going in with me whether I liked it or not. Truth be told, that had me feeling grateful. I was proud she wanted to be with me, and I felt more secure with her in the room. Even I realized I wasn't in a clear frame of mind.

It is rather peculiar how we think that while our children are young, we are taking care of this wonderful child, while all along we may be actually bringing up our own **caretaker**. This is just one more reason why we should treat them with tender loving care.

Roy stayed back with Michael. I'm certain that helped Michael feel better, especially since his mom went in with me.

As we waited for Lea to arrive, a thick cloud of apprehension hovered over both of us. We only exchanged small talk while we waited. I almost jumped when that infamous knock came upon the door. Not realizing what was about to happen had my whole existence on edge. The PA entered with a pleasant voice, "Hello, I'm Lea, the Physician Assistant. You must be Mindy's mom."

With a wide smile and sense of pride, I replied, "Yes, I am."

Looking down at the clipboard, she continued, "Mindy told me what had taken place, but I'd like to hear the story from you. She tells me you have bruises and cuts, but you don't know how you got them, is that right? May I see them?"

Without thinking, my brain knew it was time to go to the secret file. Thus, I blurted out the story about the beams, music, and voices, while I showed her the marks. She listened intently, never once acting shocked, while gently checking for tenderness on my body. When she saw the bruise on my upper arm, she said with a strong validation, "That is quite a large bruise. You say you don't know how it got there?"

"No, I don't know and that's why I'm here. I don't remember falling or bumping into anything. And I can't understand how that can happen. How can someone get bruises, cuts, and scrapes like these and not know what happened?"

"Nothing appears to be broken. However, I am concerned that you say you have been hearing music and voices." With raised brows she inquired, "How does your head feel right now?"

With a shrug, as though it were a question, I said, "Its fine?" All the while I was asking myself, *Why is she checking if my head hurts?*

"Well, I believe Mrs. LaRose, you had a seizure and that is why you are not remembering things that happened. You probably fell when you had the seizure and that is how you got so scraped up and bruised."

With a question in my voice and a frown on my brow I said, "What? A **seizure**?" With a small sense of relief, *That explains a lot. But what now?* The obvious question came up in my mind, *Do I have epilepsy?* As much as having a seizure surprised me, I was not frightened or alarmed. My father had epilepsy. I was fully aware that seizures by themselves were not life threatening. However, my brain was just cognizant enough to understand the implications. Having seizures can turn our lives upside down!

Between all my thoughts, Mindy cried out in a very surprised and sad voice, "Mom, you didn't say anything about hearing music and voices before!" Mindy's blue eyes filled with tears.

Lea looked at Mindy, "Do you need some tissues? Why aren't there any tissues in these rooms when we need them?" With concern for her friend and co-worker, she reassured her. "Don't worry, your mom is in good hands, and we will take very good care of her."

Lea then addressed me with deep benevolence. "You know, Mrs. LaRose, you have a wonderful daughter. She takes very good care of all of us here."

Then the floodgates opened for me, and tears flowed down both of our faces. Mine were not tears for me. They were tears from a mother's pride.

"You two must stop that crying before you make me cry." Now with a slight quiver in her voice she said, "I'll go find some tissues." as she left the room.

Returning a few moments later toting a box of tissues, her voice had resumed a professional and serious tone. "Mrs. LaRose, you have to go immediately to the hospital emergency department for further evaluation. We will call ahead so they will be expecting you. I'll give you both a few minutes." Once again, she left.

Mindy and I hugged, holding each other tightly as we cried. And although I was crying, I had no idea why. I should have been concerned or scared, but I wasn't. My mind was still not functioning properly. Trying to reassure each other everything was going to be fine we told each other "I love you!"

Catching our breath and gathering some of our composure, we left the room. I headed to the waiting room while Mindy returned to the front desk. Both of us had no choice but to accept what was just revealed, as well as what was about to be discovered.

As I entered the waiting room Roy saw my puffy tear-stained face and realized it was not going to be good news. He stiffened with apprehension as he asked, "What did they say?"

"She told me I had a seizure and that was why I could not remember what had happened. And we need to go immediately to the emergency department at the hospital for further evaluation."

The blood drained from Roy's face and he instantly went into autopilot. The people in the waiting room who heard this became even more somber, as the breath in the room was taken away. Roy stood up and asked in a commanding voice, "Which hospital did you say?"

I repeated the name as my demeanor took on a happy-go-lucky, drunken feel. Michael said nothing, he just followed Roy like a soldier following his commanding officer. We all walked in silence to the car.

As I left, I turned back and told Mindy, "I LOVE YOU," and with total conviction, "Everything will be fine."

"I love you too, Mom. Call me as soon as you hear anything!" She turned her head away so I could not see her cry. If she had found out any information ahead of time or even suspected something, she never told me. Like a true professional, she carried on with her duties.

I was not alarmed. Neither her tears nor Roy's stiff apprehension caused me concern. My mood was that of a child again. With my mind's functions still running wild, the atmosphere seemed to be adventuresome, one in which I was unaware of where we were going, but the anticipation was exciting. *It is just a fun day, taking a leisurely ride on a nice summer day.*

Conversation with Roy was of little consequence because he was in stealth mode. He was carrying out the mission the PA gave him: "Drive immediately to the emergency department for further evaluation."

He was sent to find out what the secret was inside of me, the one that should not be talked about. Perhaps some of this had brought back bad memories of his previous wife's experience, whom he had lost to breast cancer. This might have been leading him to be more concerned to know the secret within.

Fearful or not, it didn't matter, soon we will all know why all the odd behavior was occurring.

5

The Full Reveal

The Emergency waiting room felt eerily empty. As we looked around to find a seat, an attendant brought me a wheelchair. I wondered how he knew that I was the, sick one. He wheeled me to the front desk where a young lady asked me a few questions. Nonchalantly, I explained that Urgent Care had sent us. She looked at her computer screen, then at me, and quickly turned backed again to her screen. In a soft voice she said, "You are all set," motioning us to the double-doors. "You can go straight into the emergency ward."

My gut instantly constricted, and my instincts told me something very horrendous was about to happen. *Oh shit, shit, not good…not good at all!* It was like preparing for an audience with the *Wizard of Oz*…And I was the Cowardly Lion. That was when I jumped out the window. Although just symbolically, I disappeared, since emotionally and mentally I was no longer available. The anxiety was so intense, there is no memory of what took place after going through those doors. Without warning, Roy had to become my eyes, ears, and mind, and he lingered oblivious to that fact. It was like sleepwalking–I could move and even talk but I was not aware of anything **I** was doing. To this day, I still have no memory of what transpired next.

Months later, when I asked what happened, Roy told me, "That was when they asked you to change into a hospital gown and said they would be right back to take you up for an MRI." Hence, without knowledge of my own actions, I changed into the hospital gown, went for an MRI, and waited.

In contrast to that moment, the next thing I remember is eternally burned into my memory. That is when the tall, friendly blonde came into the room. He had such a young face, *He can't possibly be the doctor.*

He spoke in a shy voice. "So, how does your head feel now?"

With a shrug of the shoulder and a shake of my head I replied, "Fine." In more of a question than a statement.

With his tone more professional, he slowly asked, "No headache?"

Puzzled, I said, "No." But my mind was questioning, *Why does everyone keep asking me how my head feels?*

It was obvious that something was distracting him. As he hemmed and hawed, I thought he was going to tell us everything was fine, and I could go home now. What I got instead was the shock of my life.

"Well…I have good news; you did **not** have a stroke."

He then backed up to the wall with a hint of a smile on his face he slid down into a crouched position as though playing. He lingered there for a short moment. Then using his hand to push off from the floor, slowly ascended back to his full height. He hesitated again, as though he hated to give us the diagnosis. Taking a deep breath, in a delicate but faster manner, he announced …"However,…you have a brain tumor!"

His demeanor became more poised and calm now that the words had finally left his lips. "That is what caused your seizure."

My face and thoughts all froze in a questioning expression. I sat up with a blank stare, not wanting to listen anymore. I kind of felt bad for him, because he must have made a mistake. I shook my head no, because he had to be wrong, or had I heard him wrong?

Roy told me (months later), that was when Chad, Roy's son, rushed Michael out of the room. Which although I am grateful, he did that, I had no idea they had been in the room with us.

Looking at him intently, I blurted out a slow, aggressive, "Whhhaaat!?" "What did you say?" Then in a more commanding voice, "Noooo!!" As though by the power of my will, it would all be a mistake. I certainly had not required it to be repeated as it was echoing in my head, "B r a i n t u m o r!" The words echoed over and over, bouncing around like a ball in a pinball machine.

Yet, he repeated it. "You have a brain tumor." Slowing down he continued, "In fact, you actually have two brain tumors." Then, in a much quicker pace, he declared, "One is the size of a golf ball on the front temporal lobe and needs to be removed immediately. The other is in an inoperable spot and is extremely small. They are both very slow growers, and you probably had the larger one for more than twenty years."

It was a good thing Roy had been sitting, because he just had the wind knocked out of him. He choked out, "WHY A FREAKING BRAIN TUMOR?" Then he stammered out, "HOW THE HELL DID THAT HAPPEN?" as though there was someone or something to blame. The doctor gave no answer, as there really wasn't a conclusive response.

The doctor then continued his explanation, "The larger one is an olfactory groove meningioma, named that because of its location. It needs to be removed immediately." Those words are **scorched into my brain!** "We are going to keep you in the hospital for further observation. All scheduled surgeries are done on Thursdays."

Once more I went blank. There is no further memory except them telling me they wanted to keep me for more tests. My mother was right, "Always be sure to have clean underwear on because you never know what might happen to you!"

With my heart in my throat and my brain in a state of shock, I just stared out into space. No correct connections were being made. All sensible thoughts refused to register. If they had told me I had a stroke, like my brother Jim had, or breast cancer like my two sisters had, I would not have been so stunned. But, a Brain Tumor! How could that be? How could I not know it or feel it? I never had any bad headaches. Like a short circuit, my brain was flickering on and off.

The last thought I remembered was, *I need to have brain surgery*! *A Craniotomy. A word which I am not sure I am even pronouncing correctly*! My brain shut down. Its circuitry could not take any more…lights out.

6

·······

Reminiscing Turns into Mental Gymnastics

I started recalling the bad experiences I had that brought me to the hospital, in fact, reflecting became a permanent state of mind in between all the tests:-EEG,-EKG,-CAT Scans, and more intensive-MRIs. With each test, I wanted to ask all sorts of questions, but I didn't know what to ask. Plus, fear was clouding my judgement. Instead I joked around and pretended I wasn't frightened. Once I was back in the room with my own thoughts, I reflected and questioned why I had all those terrifying hallucinations and exhibited that odd behaviors. *Yes, I realized I had the tumor, but what caused me to **feel** the intense beating from the beams, and hear the music that stopped them? And, what about the apparition in the mirror? Why did I see and feel all of that horror? Was I supposed to find meaning in any of that? Had the tumors caused me to go crazy?* Those episodes weighed heavy on my mind and in my soul. However, I couldn't handle another ounce of bad news, so I bottled-up my thoughts.

Switching my thoughts, I began reflecting about family that had already departed this life. I had been there for my parents and two of the four siblings as they declined. I was completely aware the only thing I could do was help them feel comfortable as they departed. I had no control to stop it. I watched, held hands with, and nurtured my parents as they slowly deteriorated—one from cirrhosis of the liver, the other from prostate cancer, both almost reaching their 90th birthday. The sad reality was all I could do was pensively observed their bodies slowly weaken before death overtook them. All the while knowing without them, we would no longer be able to talk to each other, share our love, or touch. During those moments, it pushed me in two different emotional directions. One was closer to them and the other was a safe distance for self-preservation, knowing without them…I would be extremely broken-hearted for a long time. Those memories left me wondering, were these the reactions they felt when they dealt with their own passing. That, emotional state of mind, made it difficult <u>not</u> to think about my own demise. That triggered me to feel more isolated. I had to stop this sadness. Wanting to be stronger and less frightened pushed me to refocus.

Attempting to keep my mind calm and occupied, I chose to think about happier times. I started by bringing in memories of my younger life. I recalled our huge holiday parties and joyful picnics. Those gatherings were substantial due to the sheer size of our family of ten, certainly not the size of the dwelling we lived in. Growing up, we usually lived in very small apartments. That took me to the time when I was only four years old.

By the time I was four, half of my siblings were already married with children of their own. Hence, the immediate family I grew up with was smaller in size. We lived in a small village, above an appliance store, in the center of town. It was, at most, 800 sq. ft., with only two-and one-half bedrooms.

That was where our now smaller family of six lived. Mom and Dad's room was not the largest bedroom because they needed to give that to their three daughters, RoseALee (age 14), JoAnne (AKA Annie, age 7), and me (age 4). Our brother Jim (age 10), slept in a converted hallway closet. It was similar the one Harry Potter slept in, in the novel; <u>Harry Potter and the Philosopher's Stone</u>. I dare not forget the hallway between Jim's bedroom and the kitchen, because that was our only playroom. The fact that we lived on Main Street, in the center of town, made it our only safe play area.

This particular day we decided to play hospital. Jimmy had recently had his tonsils removed and I think he wanted to show us what had happened to him. Jimmy wanted to be the doctor, Annie was the nurse, and I was the patient. It began by searching for a pretend hospital bed. Somehow, the idea came to Jim that placing two chairs face to face would work as that bed. He suggested we use the new rocking chairs we just received for Christmas. I remember thinking, he must be a genius, a world class inventor, to think of that. Now, these rocking chairs weren't *just* a new Christmas gift. They were our only gift, other than maybe a baby doll and some new clothes. We loved them, especially since our father built them. Well, it was more like he assembled them. They were wooden with a cozy curved seat for our buttocks and two horizontal rails for our backs. Dad even carved our names and the date on the rails using a wood-burning tool. They were extra special to all of us! And they turned out to be the perfect size for our hospital bed, or so we thought.

After lying down, I realized those curves meant to make one's buttock fit nicely, were not good for lying on, because they were very hard and wavy. So, we put a pillow on them for cushioning, which helped make them feel more like a bed. Despite our efforts those rockers made a very short bed, even for a four-year-old. So, Jimmy came up with another idea, "Put your head under the bottom rail so you can fit." I had complete confidence in his suggestion, especially since he was so smart and already ten years old.

However, shortly after stuffing my head under the rail, I realized my head was stuck! No matter how hard I wiggled, I was STUCK! The pillows left no room to maneuver, and they were impossible to remove because I was lying on them. Jimmy thought it was funny, so I laughed too. The more I struggled, the more he laughed.

The whole mood changed very quickly, when I heard Jimmy say, "We'll probably have to cut you out!" I thought he meant they would have to cut my head off! So, I started to scream and cry! Annie got scared too, and she started to cry with me. Jimmy just continued to laugh. Then, with a little compassionate giggle he explained, "The rail is going to be cut off, not your head…you big crybabies!"

Then Annie got angry because it was her chair my head was stuck in. I still remember what I was thinking, *If only my head was stuck in my rocker instead.* I was in red hot trouble for sure! But I did not know what to fear more: Annie or what Mom was going to do to us for wrecking the new rocker.

Big brother Lou was the one who came to my rescue. He was armed with a saw in one hand and a towel in the other. The towel was to cover my face and eyes. Although the towel was a great idea, it didn't stop me from screaming! (I could almost hear Jim laughing as I reminisced in my hospital bed. It brought a grin to my face, even after all these years.)

The memory of that experience had me smiling and thinking, what a wonderful childhood I had. And although we may not have had a lot of stuff, we had love and knew we could be rescued. *How ironic that I should think of that story while waiting for brain surgery.* Perhaps it was because Jim is no longer with us.

Reminiscing was certainly bittersweet. The distraction was helpful, and it had me yearning for the simple lost times of my youth, like those times when I was surrounded by the protection of my siblings. I have no desire to be this mature adult, facing this potentially life-threatening surgery. I wanted to be that little girl rescued by her big brother once more.

Something jarred me back to reality. *Oh crap, I won't be able to take the job I was hired for. I need to call the staffing company and tell them what is happening.* That means Roy might not be able to retire when he wants, especially since he is the one with the medical insurance.

Then other thoughts poured in. *How am I ever going to get a job now? I might not be able to ever work again after surgery.*

Deep inside, I felt the necessity to find a way to clean-up my thought process to stop this inner turmoil.

7

In an Emotional Washing Machine

Doctor S (the neurosurgeon) told me, when they remove the tumor, my ability to smell and most of my ability to taste will be gone. Since I had lost most of those senses already, from the tumor, it was not much of an issue to me. Despite that fact being acceptable to me, the issue(s) of the unknown were still lingering.

While contemplating my situation, my mind began wondering about our family's life expectancy again. At one point I had assumed there was longevity in our genes. That was evident since both sets of my grandparents and my parents lived into their late eighties. On the contrary, my siblings indicated that fact might not necessarily be accurate. Losing four siblings when they were approximately the age I am now, had me thinking quite differently. *Was I next to leave the family?* was front and center in my thoughts.

Alone late at night, the uncertainties crept in causing moisture from my eyes to stream down my cheeks and neck. Like soft raindrops after a hot steamy day, my teardrops were trying to reassure me everything was going to be fine. However, with my emotions so twisted, there was no good way to convince me everything would ever be normal again. Every possible scenario was playing out in my head, and all of them caused more torment.

Nothing in life even came close to preparing me for this. One of the worst parts was feeling foolish and uncomfortable asking questions like: "Will I be able to do x, y, or z after surgery? More accurately, I really didn't want to talk to anyone about it. A part of me was afraid to hear or know what was to come. For perhaps the first time in my life, I wanted to be left completely alone. I knew this was something only I could deal with because the dread was within **my** head. Even if someone had tried to help, it wouldn't have done any good. No one could change this.

This situation became a large spinning cycle in my mind. My thoughts were in an emotional washing machine, trying to wash all the bad news down the drain. The right side of my brain had been swished against the left side, as the left side whirled around the right, as both sides swirled against me. The terrified child within cried out for strength, *Look what is happening to me; Mama help me!* The strong woman within yelled out, *what are you doing to yourself? You're a strong woman! You know how to be strong, get up and fight! You do want to live, don't you? Then prove it!* For two days, that emotional washing machine was tossing me around attempting to cleanse my thoughts. When the spinning ceased, I was back to the real world in the hospital room. I had completely exhausted myself from all the mental cycles. Time to sleep, knowing there was now less than forty-eight hours until surgery. Although not happy, I felt I had finally reached a place of acceptance and was ready to face my unwanted fate. Perhaps it was the meds taking effect that finally calmed my whirling thoughts.

Upon waking the next morning, I was in a better frame of mind. I had convinced myself to look forward to the time I had left on this earth, regardless of the length. Putting that fresh frame of mind into action caused some patients and their visitors to probably think I was completely insane, but I didn't care. I was desperately trying to stay upbeat for everyone, including myself. But to no one's surprise, I took it too far. I acted like I was happy by clowning around while they wheeled me down the halls for more tests. I smiled and waved to the other patients as though I was being paraded around to bring them laughter. I acted out that way, to spread some love, or at least a smile. Surprisingly, all that love came streaming back. It became an additional accelerant that helped me to be emotionally ready for the surgery. However, things do not always happen as planned.

On Wednesday, Doctor S the neurosurgeon, came in to talk to me. His 6' 3" slender frame towered over my 5' 4" shortness. Both physically and emotionally his demeanor commanded confidence, keeping me more grounded. With a half-smile, he greeted me, "Good morning, how is your head feeling today? Are you in any pain?"

"I am doing well, thank you. My head is fine, it doesn't hurt at all. Could you please explain why I don't remember some of the events that happened to me and why I had such terrifying hallucinations?"

He looked at me inquisitively, as though I had forgotten I had a seizure from the brain tumor. Nonetheless, he began explaining. "You have a tumor which caused you to have a seizure. A seizure can cause electrical activity in the brain. Certain electrical activity disrupts normal function of the brain and spreads." At that point, I felt I was in for a lonnnggg drawn out medical narrative. All I heard was the faint sound of his voice as it gradually drifted away.

"But we do know… blah, blah, blah and processing emotions. Seizures in this blah, blah…joy, recall of certain music, and other…"

That explanation caused more confusion in me. It did not explain what I was really trying to comprehend. I smiled and said, "thank you" but felt, *I should have asked my question differently, but I wasn't sure how to put it into words.*

Interjecting his own thoughts, he smiled and continued with his main purpose for the visit, "All of the test results are in and everything is pointing to benign tumors, just as we had suspected. The test also revealed there are NO other brain tumors any place else in your body. You can go home tomorrow."

My bulging eyes must have been all telling as they opened wider with alarm! And, my thoughts screamed so loud in my head I think he heard them! *What the——do you mean, I can go home TOMORROW?* **What?** *Are you not removing the tumor??!!*

He must have **realized** he said something that bothered me deeply. With an almost apologetic voice, he continued, "Of course, you will have to return on Thursday the 21st for your scheduled surgery."

In an attempt to show gratitude, instead of the absolute shock I really felt, I said calmly, "OH…Thank God for no other tumors!" Although, still in shock, I continued to hold my composure. "But how could you tell they were benign and what do you mean no other '**brain**' tumors anyplace else in my body?"

Nonchalantly, (as though I was ignorant) he replied, "Well, tumors can be anyplace in the body, so we needed to find out if the tumors came from another place within your body or if they were spread throughout. We found they are only located in one area, your head. As for how we know they are benign, that was done through all the tests. One of the MRI tests sliced into the larger tumor and it was looked at from all angles. Now, that is not 100%, but everything is pointing in that direction. We will also do a biopsy after we remove it to be absolutely certain there is no cancer."

One might think that was all great news, and most of it was. All of it, actually, except…that one gigantic statement about me going home without having the surgery. My heart and body stiffened with anxiety when he said those words.

The prospect of being home alone and repeating what just happened last week had me still filled with terror. Post-trauma panic seized me. A part of me just wanted to run and hide, *I don't want to go home. In fact, I am petrified to go home!* For the first time in my life, home was no longer "home sweet home" especially knowing that I would be alone again. I had finally convinced myself I was ready to have this tumor removed, and I needed the surgery done now. How could they possibly expect me to be okay with waiting another week?

I began to feel like a child on a never-ending emotional roller coaster…with ebbs and flows which could not be predicted or controlled.

The doctor merely stood there pensively looking at me. He realized he had said something that disturbed me but didn't know what it was or what to say next. "Of course, you will have to be on a 24/7 watch when you go home. You do have someone that can be with you?"

I lied, "Yes."

It was simply a word for him to hear, and for me to move beyond my frustrations. He left the room, maybe suspecting the truth but not saying another word. It became necessary, after taking it all in, for me to face facts. Time to reprocess everything again.

When Roy came in to visit, I asked if he would take some time off work and stay home with me. As I told him the news, his voice filled with hesitation, "We will just have to make arrangements to have someone with you while you are home. If I must, I'll take some days off. Or…you can ask your brother Louie to come over for a few days. Somehow, we will work this out."

It was my older brother Louie who came to my rescue once again. He was my comfort, my sounding board. Our conversations were filled with emotion as we talked and cried, then talked some more. He helped me to face my fears and understand what the other family members were going through.

8

Research Tiptoed in Like a Herd of Elephants

While waiting for Louie to arrive, the preoccupation to research brain surgery tiptoed into my head like a herd of elephants. One of the forewarnings that came up time and time again was, "Patients might need to prepare **for extreme pain!"** Reading that did not alarm me, but it placed me on alert. What really intimidated me were the pictures, the ones that showed the patient *clamped* down with the three prong steel tentacles holding the head to the operating table, like a piece of wood in a vise grip! It brought back memories of the time I had watched a craniotomy being performed on television. I had been so amazed and curious while watching how they drilled and sawed into a skull to remove that tumor. But now, **now**…someone will be drilling into *my* skull. This time, they are taking a piece of *my* skull bone, putting it aside, so they could pull the tumor out of me. Curiosity and amazement were no longer on my mind. Uncertainties lived there now.

What that TV program failed to show was the recovery, or what the family might have to deal with. I had to mentally run away, because it was all too harsh to face. However, like sobering up after a night of partying, eventually like it or not–reality brought me right back to face the cold, hard facts. I began to imagine what my family might need to be prepared for or what they might have to go through. The need to also understand their circumstances and what had already happened pushed me to do additional research. All my memory loss and why I had the terrifying hallucinations haunted me. What I found out helped me to understand my odd, unexplainable behavior.

The following is only a snapshot of what I learned from: https://www.epilepsy.com/learn/about-epilepsy-basics/what-happens-during-seizure

The information below helped me:

- Seizures can take on many different forms and affect different people differently.
- Every person with seizures will not have every stage or symptom.

Early warning symptoms (called an aura) are the onset of a seizure and may stop on its own or go on to spread, producing **altered awareness.**

- **Some Physical Changes** – (some happened to me)

Awareness, Sensory, Emotional, or Thought Changes:

- Slow to respond or not able to respond right away
- Sleepy
- Confused
- Memory loss
- Difficulty talking or writing
- Feeling fuzzy, lightheaded, or dizzy
- Feeling depressed, sad, upset
- Scared
- Anxious
- Frustrated

Physical Changes: – (some happened to me)

- May have injuries, such as bruising, cuts, broken bones, or head injury if you fell during seizure
- May feel tired, exhausted, or sleep for minutes or hours
- Nausea or upset stomach
- General weakness

I learned that some of this behavior is seen in temporal lobe epileptics who often describe undergoing spiritual out-of-body events during seizures.

This information helped me understand more and feel much better about myself. It emphasized to me I wasn't insane or going insane. My behavior, all the hallucinations, and everything else that had occurred, could be explained and was normal "for this condition".

9

••••••

Signs I Had Ignored

The knowledge obtained from researching seizures had me thinking about the symptoms that I ignored for various reasons. Yet, even after reflecting, not a single warning sign hinted I had anything growing within my skull, but several should have. They appeared as little whispers within, and they gradually grew. Due to their disguise as a stomach issue or a mood swing / anxiety, plus the hiatus of time between each physical occurrence, two and two never equaled brain tumor for me. I excused them all as symptoms of old age, not as warnings.

Looking back, I could recall how anxiety came on so quickly and so easily. Just hearing certain sounds, like a motorcycle revving (especially when I was trying to study) caused me to be anxious. It kept me from concentrating on anything except for what seemed like a loud obnoxious roar from a damned motor. That noise caused my whole body to become so anxious it made me tremble. All I could think about, when I heard it, was getting the damn thing out of the entire neighborhood. It wasn't that I hated them. I used to enjoy motorcycles. In fact, I rode on the back of one for many years. I often rode with a group of friends; we would go camping on weekends and ride on logging trails when I was in my twenties. But at this phase, things changed, something was very different about the noise they made.

What could have been one of the first physical warning sign came on about three years prior to my diagnosis. I was driving to work, wishing that I didn't have to go because it was such a beautiful day. Presto, my wish came true! Out of the clear blue, a stomach spasm signaled me to pull over immediately to avoid having vomit in my van. Shocked over what was happening, I quickly turned into a nearby housing track and expelled it all on someone's manicured lawn. It came out in one large explosion. Baffled, embarrassed, and now late for work, I considered the fact, *I don't even feel sick, what was that all about!* Despite everything, more accurately in addition to it all, I felt humiliated and wished for rain so the mess could be washed away.

While attempting to find a reason, I searched my memory for what I had eaten the night before. But I came up with nothing out of the ordinary that should have provoked vomiting. So, I shook it off and went to work. Since I was late, I mentioned the incident to my boss. He gave me "the look", the one when someone thinks they caught you lying. In mid-sentence and without warning, as though rehearsed and staged, I proceeded to vomit right in front of him! Luckily, I was able to whirl my chair around just in time to deposit it into the trash bin. Stunned and wide eyed…he shouted out, "GO HOME, go home NOW!"

Not knowing what was developing had me concerned about being home alone, but I really had no other good choice. Less than a mile down the road, it occurred again. Each time there was little to no gagging involved, just a quick warning, and an evil explosion. This time I was too exhausted to care about it being washed away.

Once I got home the vomiting stopped, but I was exhausted and went to bed. When Roy got home, we went to Urgent Care to try to find out what the issue was. The PA suggested it might be a kidney stone. He told me there really was nothing he could do, that the stone would have to pass. He handed me a strainer to collect it. *Oh boy, how great is that? I not only get to vomit all morning; I get to catch the culprit that caused it.* After all of this…I either did not have a stone or it slipped out undetected. The next day all was normal again, as though nothing strange had occurred. Instead of a kidney stone, I now wonder if that episode might have been the first physical sign.

The next occurrence was about six months later, when I tripped at work and fell into the wall. I fell to the left as I rushed down the hall. The odd part was…the wall came <u>alive</u>. It literally attempted to catch me. Tiny gnome sized appendages reached out vigorously to prevent me from falling. The hands mimicked my every oscillating movement. For the next four to five steps, I wobbled back and forth but didn't fall because the wall / hands caught me. Once I was stable, I just stood motionless for a full minute, completely frozen, not wanting to look at anything, (especially the wall). Flabbergasted and filled with disbelief over what had occurred, I simply walked away. I never told a soul about the incident because it was so damned peculiar. Instead of questioning what that was all about, I simply rationalized it as a vivid imagination.

By November, of 2009, my cognitive thoughts and emotions had sorely begun to fail me. Although I hadn't noticed it yet, my bosses had. Like a lot of companies during that time period, the software company where I was working had been failing, which led to several layoffs. Since I made it through several of those purges, I thought I was safe. However, things began to feel quite different when, not one, but <u>three</u> of my bosses came to me and asked me to do something on the Internet. My mind went completely blank, I just stared at the screen. It was as though they asked me to perform a miracle. I choked. I merely could not give them what they asked for. Shortly after that incident, I was laid off.

To keep my spirits up after that fiasco, I pushed myself to do something good. I seized the opportunity to pursue my lifelong dream to finish my degree. January 2010, I was exploring the classes, books, and events at our nearby college. Most of that was pleasurable and uneventful except for a few minor incidents, like that one day after gym class when I felt a little dizzy, queasy, and out of sorts. I was in the hallway, near the nurse's office, asking myself whether I was ill enough to seek medical care. I could feel my subconscious pushing me to go in, (given that the office being right in front of me). The nurse was nonchalant, as I had expected her to be, since I had no outward physical symptoms. She told me, "Perhaps you are just a little stressed."

However, mysteriously I started to feel better. I asked her if they had oxygen pumping into her office. She looked at me curiously and told me that they did have fresh air pumped in. Then she looked at me with a question in her eyes and asked, "Why are you asking?"

I took in another deep breath, "Because for some reason I feel better than when I first came in." This incident had me pondering about the cause, but again there really wasn't anything substantial to complain about.

Over the next year, between 2010 and 2011, episodes occurred more frequently. Each episode was a little different than the previous one. Some came on in restaurants; even before we ordered our food, nausea was triggered. And even in my favorite place (my garden) heat exhaustion caused me to seek shelter. One Saturday morning, the garden became the location of a flare-up. I could not pull another weed or deadhead another flower even though I had only been out there less than a half hour. This episode was so harsh, I had to lie myself down or pass out... in the dirt. There I was lying in the garden, weak as a newborn kitten, *I'm just a little over-heated, though I don't know why. I'll be fine if I just lie here for a moment.* But it didn't help much, so I headed inside to an air-conditioned room. On a beautiful, sunny, Saturday morning, I was lying semi-exhausted on the couch feeling like a lazy teenager. Conversely, it was a whole lot better than feeling like a sick, old grandma. My grandson Michael watch over me. He fussed over me like adults do when they are taking care of a sick child.

The dilemma was, none of those symptoms, by themselves, were cause enough to make an appointment with a doctor. With each flareup, I had already forgotten about the previous one. It was only in hindsight that I realized there could have been possible connected warning signs. Nevertheless, as is obvious to me now, my inner being was keeping copious notes.

Despite the research and the identifying of symptoms, it was not any easier for me to face the surgical knife. However, it should be mentioned, due to the week of medication in the hospital, my brain/emotions were working more appropriately. Even though the circumstances had not changed, I was functioning more realistically. My thinking was clearer, and my emotions were reacting more on par. Yes, I still had a fear-provoking situation to face, but now I was reacting to a real situation, not horrifying hallucinations.

10

• • • • • •

The Surgery Could NOT be Stopped

Thursday, June 21st, 2012, 4:45 AM, Roy and I prepared to go to the hospital. Barely a word was spoken between us. I lingered in numbness, finding it difficult to even move one foot in front of the other. As the seconds ticked by, all the risks I was facing engulfed my mind…all sorts of negative thoughts ran rampant, as though they were in a race, each one wanting to be the first to grab my attention. One of the scary parts of brain surgery is…I might make it through the surgery. *What will our life be like if I do? Would Roy ever want to look at me again? Will I want to look at myself?* My mind played out all the scenarios I had been trying to ignore. *I know he loves me, but would I be the same person?*

One of the overwhelming parts of this journey was dealing with those mixed emotions, especially the ones associated with potential death. It was not that I hadn't dealt with death, I had. I dealt very closely with two of my four siblings and my parents all passing. And I knew, not even the best doctors, the best-known medicine, and all the prayers in the world could stop death. And of course, trying to properly prepare for the possibility of my own death was more difficult. As many people have said, there are no rules, road maps, or emotions within life that can help you prepare. It is an extremely sad and lonely place. Even if I had felt closer to the Lord, it would still be hard to leave. I would no longer be able to see, touch, or hug my loved ones. It left me feeling powerless and full of questions that had no answers. *Would we really meet all who have passed before us? Or would we just end...period!* Either way, I was not ready to know. What I did know was, I wanted to remain right here for and with my family.

All of this had me pushing for positive thoughts so I could be strong for my family and myself. Preparing in silence, holding my family close to my heart, helped me to maintain a more composed demeanor even while sadness tiptoed in. It was now necessary to reboot (kick myself in the ass). The "poor me" attitude and negativity had to go. Time to summon help from the highest power. I silently prayed that the doctors were not only totally experienced, but that they were EXCELLENT at performing brain surgery, along with a smaller, selfish, prayer that they had some sense that most women have an inherent want to look presentable. I know that latter request was foolish, but...it was on my mind and it gave me hope of survival.

That prayer ignited a happy thought within me. *This could be like a spring cleaning of the brain...giving me a better brain. It might even give me a mini face lift.* Finally, I found an emotional happy place where only I could go. These thoughts lifted my spirits and increased my confidence in hopes of survival. Always keeping God in my heart and soul helped me to put one foot in front of the other, so I could show the world, like many others that had gone before me––it can be done. I too, can survive a craniotomy.

11

•••••••

The Light of God

Once at the hospital, there was very little time to think about anything, let alone have bad thoughts. Plus, I had done such a good job going to my happy place that I had a grand time in pre-op. That seems strange, yet it was true. I was enthusiastic and happy, and I'm sure some of the drugs they had given me played a big part in this euphoria. As more visitors came to show their support, a deep sense of gratitude came over me. Knowing my immediate family had support overwhelmed me with peace and gratitude.

A much younger lady lying in another bed was wheeled into the holding area. Even though I had no idea what type of operation she was preparing for, my heart reached out to her. I overheard the nurse ask her, "So what movie did you watch last night to bring you to a happy place?" And I thought, *That's a really good idea. I wish I had done that.* Then I said a prayer for her.

Everyone was saying how brave I was as I laid there in the hospital garb. It had me smiling as I thought of myself in a ceremonial gown and head-dress. (pictures in appendix A)

It conjured up an image within me. I felt like I was preparing for a transformation, to prove my true strength as an adult. Happily, I said my goodbyes to everyone as though I were just going for a walk. I kissed Roy and Mindy, and told them, "I love you, see you both when I wake up." Almost instantly, I fell asleep. I have no memory of anything past that point.

When asked, both Roy and Mindy said, the operation including recovery took approximately eight hours. The average surgical time required for craniotomy is anywhere from 4 to 6 hours.

Unlike previous surgeries I have gone through, I experienced a vision this time. Since I had no concept of time, I sensed it happened in the recovery room. It started when I heard commotion, and my surgeon's voice bellow out in a loud concerned tone. He shouted something about the amount of anesthesia was too much. Then silence…complete silence. Despite that, what happened next was *extremely beautiful!* I was in a daze as I woke and heard the doctor's voice. Opening my eyes, I didn't see much of my surroundings except what was above me. Slightly to my right was a glowing circular portal. The opening floated only over my face, which led me to feel it isn't something one should enter. It stayed approximately two feet in diameter, hovering in midair. Its center was pitch-black with a white halo surrounding the circumference as it illuminated outward like a solar eclipse. I was not anxious, nor felt as though I was dying. Its presence gave me **absolute peace, it grounded me**. My whole being was filled with amazement and ecstasy. That is when, I heard **my own voice**, responding to what the doctor had just said. In a gentle yet firm tone, I told everyone in earshot, "There is no need to worry. **GOD** is with me! Everything will be okay." Those were my exact words, for I believed that Beam of Light was a sign that all was well. I felt as though I had experienced a profound event, a spiritual blessing. I witnessed, what felt like "**The Light of God**".

Total calm washed within and throughout me and the room. Then, once again, complete silence…complete obscurity.

To this day I have unanswered questions and doubts in my mind. *Why was the center pitch black? Why did I feel I was not supposed to go through it? Was it a premonition? Perhaps it was a vital foretelling; showing me what was needed to bring about my recovery.* My mind kept swimming with questions. I didn't feel that was a bad omen because I felt at peace with it. The only true knowledge I had was…I survived. With all the theatrics aside, this truly felt like a transformation process had begun. What I was experiencing was very strange, but at the same time I thought *HOW BEAUTIFUL AND WONDERFUL!* The Catholics call it a "Beatific Vision".

The next thing I remember, Roy and Mindy were greeting me with warm smiles in the intensive care unit (ICU). They each greeted me with whispers, "How do you feel?" It was as though they were concerned about hurting me. I had no pain at all, and my spirit was filled with joy. I was alive, alive with pleasure that I was going to see them for another day and hopefully many years to come. In my heart and mind, I wanted to dance, but my body was content just to lie still…and smile.

Almost instantly, I told them about my vision, and they only looked at me with amazement.

Mindy asked, "Had you ask the doctor if anything happened during surgery?"

"I haven't seen him yet." was my only response.

But it would not matter. I don't believe anything odd happened during surgery. As far as I was concerned, it wouldn't matter if anyone else saw anything. I knew what I had experienced and witnessed.

Time to move onto recovery, and I was up to the challenge. However, even though I felt ready, my body wasn't.

12

••••••

On the "Trip" to Recovery

Recovery began in the ICU, a typical hospital room nondescriptive, sterile, and designed for healing, yet it felt like a queen's bedroom. It was large enough for several visitors to come in at the same time. I was alive, had zero pain, and my attitude was happy. The room may not have been interesting, but with all the visitors it was filled with love. Everyone treated me like royalty. With time being ambiguous, especially after surgery, I have no idea how long I spent there.

Regardless, I felt good and happy in the beginning. I was rejoicing at the fact of being alive. I felt full of life and gratitude, because there was zero pain. And although I couldn't do either one very well yet...I could still think and talk. Recovery came slowly at first, and I felt pure pleasure with, any of, my progress. I laughed and joked about my unsightly new hairstyle and deformities. No doubt, I was in the state of euphoria from the medication, although I had not realized that fact at the time. It felt like the worst part was over, at least that was what I thought. I simply did not know that psychological issues were slowly edging in and would taunt me throughout the remainder of my stay.

When I was moved to a semi-private room the visits from friends and family had slowed down and I had a few moments alone. I started wondering what I truly looked like with the sutures. I became restless to know how bad my appearance was. Instead of being brave and using a mirror, I asked the young girl who delivered my lunch. "How bad does my scar look?"

As soon as the words were out of my mouth, I felt bad. I could sense I might have unintentionally frightened her. Which was obvious from her downward gaze; she did not want to look let alone respond. But she was polite and looked up. With a tiny tremor in her voice, "It really isn't terrible. I think if you put a scarf on, it won't look too bad! They left some hair for you to do a comb-over." *Ohhh swell, a comb-over! A comb-over, just great!* There was no way I wanted to see myself in a mirror now. But I needed to get past that, so I pushed harder to adapt a more positive attitude.

Even though I was hooked up to all sorts of lines, both going in and out of my body, I still felt good. Not even the drainage tube coming out of my skull bothered me much. I knew that would be removed soon. The one exception was the alarm that had me tethered to the bed. I hated that thing. ("Hated" does not quite capture the full range of my negative feelings about being restrained to the bed). From my viewpoint it became a symbol of disability. That alarm was a constant reminder that I wasn't <u>whole</u>. Even if I only needed to use the bathroom, **It** was there and told me, "Oh no, you can't do that by yourself!" The hatred for that bed alarm would present itself four or more times daily. So, I started strategizing about how I could do a work-around and prove I did NOT need the alarm. I would start out with a little "discussion" between the two sides of my brain:

The irrational side of my brain claimed, *I hate being tethered to this bed!*

The logical side would argue back, *It is for your own safety.*

Irrational: *"But I'm fine <u>physically</u>, why can't they see that it was my brain they operated on, not my legs."* Looking at the bathroom door, knowing it was only three to four feet away, I convinced myself I could reach it without help. My closing argument would be, *My bladder is so full, if I don't get to the bathroom soon, I am going to have an accident."* Then I topped it off with fun:

I'm not in pain, I'm not at my worse.
I can do this without bothering the nurse.
After all, the other patients need them more than me
For I only have to pee.

Laughing inside at myself, because I made a rhyme, I would scurry out of bed like a child at play and waddle to the bathroom. Of course, the alarm would ring out, catching me in the middle of my escape, calling for the nurses to come help me. I'd rush a little faster, (faster being a relative term) hoping to show them how well I was doing. The nurse would scold me, "You know you should call us to help you out of bed?"

"I know, but I'm fine."

They would argue back, "But if something bad <u>should</u> happen…"

But impatience continued to power my thoughts. I understood the hospital was concerned that I might black-out and get hurt. Yet despite that, like a child, I ignored their warnings. From my prospective, I had to show the world I was still alive and strong enough to do things for myself.

I was like the obstinate child who insisted on growing up faster than I was truly capable of. It became important to try to get to the bathroom alone even though my legs were weak and bowed. I even had concerns that my legs might possibly stay bent for the rest of my life and worse. Sometimes I even felt impending death. That was the most god-awful feeling…dark and gloomy…filled with loss, and no hope. That had me pushing myself harder to improve. To re-build my strength and coordination they had me walk around the nurse's station.

My first rude awakening came one night when I was heading to the bathroom with the nurse by my side. As I reached the restroom, I stopped cold in extreme terror. The nurse grabbed my arm with apprehension, "Are you alright?"

I couldn't answer. I realized I was the only one who sensed its evil existence. A dark force in the form of a billowing mass was looming above my head. I felt it wanted to take my soul causing my body to weaken and my breathing to intensify. I knew I should flee, but I was frozen by terror and couldn't. I did nothing except stand very still trying to be invisible, in hopes it would not find me. With tears now streaming down my cheeks, all I could do was ask God for help. I begged, *Please give me strength, I'm not ready to leave.* I cried out in silence, *My family still needs me.* In an instant, the strong woman within came out filled with anger that I wasn't fighting back. I closed my eyes and took a deep breath, letting the power of prayer expand my strength. Still shaking but stronger, I was now able to reply, "I just need a moment."

As I took another deep breath, she opened the door to the bathroom. As soon as the light shined on my face, the phantom vanished. With uncertainty she asked, "Are you sure you are going to be okay?"

Knowing it had left, it was easier to say, "I am better now."

After that incident, my passion to rush became a little more restrained. I was continuously repeating the same prayer under my breath: *I love my family too much to leave this soon; I want to see them all again; I can't die! My immediate family has already lost four siblings. My children have already lost their father and Roy had already lost one wife. I WON'T HURT THEM FURTHER WITH MY DEATH!* While reflecting about what had happened, I questioned, *Is this the drugs playing cruel, foolish tricks in my mind, or is this a common side effect from the brain surgery? Or am I really dying?* I tried to shake all those emotions away, but it was not always easy.

Part of this recovery trip brought with it the sharp venom of reality. Of course, that came with a message plus vengeance. My quest for a speedy recovery was about to teach me an extremely harsh lesson. The penalty was to be tenfold and brutal. The worst part, the vengeance, was placed onto my family. The only reason I deserve any forgiveness for my reckless rushing is the fact that I was utterly oblivious that my actions would hurt my family. Sure, I had been warned, "You might black out". But no one said, your actions will cause your family to suffer. Plus, I thought I had made it past the worst of this ordeal. It felt like this was the coasting into home plate time because, despite what I had read and gone through, I had little to no pain at all. Therefore, it seemed to be fun to rush about, be alive, and be playful. I could not have been more wrong! This lesson is the kind people **never** forget!

13

• • • • • • •

Drainage Tube is Removed

The removal of the drainage tube, from my skull, marked the start of the penalty I was to pay for my foolishness. Although the time frame was sketchy, at best. I remember it was rather early in the morning when two young neurosurgeon attendees, that looked like McDreamy and Dr. Sloan from "Grey's Anatomy", came into my room. They stood at the end of my bed and announced that it was time to remove the drainage tube from my skull. And although their kind demeanors and handsome faces helped me to stay calm, my internal alarms were going off. Automatically my stomach muscles tightened, and my eyes widened with anticipated fear. Their announcement had me remembering the tug I felt when the drainage tube was removed after my gallbladder surgery. That tube had become affixed to my body, which caused a pull when it was removed. This conversation caused all my thoughts to rush into one, *Will some of my brain tissue be pulled out when they remove this one?*

Simply thinking about that extraction intuitively grossed me out. I took a deep breath and asked in a meek voice, "Is this going to hurt?"

Dr. M, (McDreamy), kindly replied, "Not from what we have been told, but you will feel a tug."

With a ripple in my stomach I thought, *Oh no, a tug! That means, something is going to be attached to the other end of the tube…and that something is going to be tissue from MY BRAIN!*

My mind was racing, *Oh crap! It is definitely going to hurt!*

Both doctors smiled at me. Then Dr. S (Dr. Sloan), added calmly, "I'll tell you what, you can do us a favor. You can tell us what it felt like, after we take it out."

With a bob from my head and my eyes now bulging out, *what was meant by that? I hope to God this isn't their first time removing a tube from a skull!* Despite all of that, I gently held my breath and looked the other way. Knowing it was not going to kill me, I tried not to think about my brains being attached to the tube, (which was almost impossible to do). I felt like a scared child as I anticipated a gigantic Band-Aid being ripped off. Holding the tube gently in his hand, the doctor asked, "Are you ready?"

With my eyes closed in meditative prayer, *Please help me to be strong.* I answered, "Yes."

Instantly, I felt it slithering out. I started to gag, but before I could…It was out! *Oh, my God!* The trepidations were definitely worse than the pain. *Oh, my…Thank You… Thank You!* I became so elated, "Oh! That's it, how did you do that without it hurting? Thank you so very much!"

Trying to keep me in good spirits, the doctor replied with a smile, "It's like magic, and we are very glad there was no pain. You should rest now. We'll be back to check on your progress later today."

I wanted to hug them, but I was contented to give them a big smile to convey my gratitude. All that fear for nothing left me peacefully pacified. Since the early morning still had me groggy, sleep came back quickly, as I felt another step closer to recovery. When I woke again, I saw Roy sitting in the chair by the bed with his morning coffee and a smile. "Good morning, how are you feeling today?"

"I feel really good. How are you doing? You must be exhausted from all of this running around."

"I'm fine, you're the one I'm worried about. Have the doctors been in yet? I wanted to ask them some questions, but I keep missing them."

"They were in, and they took the drainage tube out. I thought it would really hurt, or feel gross slithering out, but it didn't. In fact, it shocked me that I barely felt it coming out."

With a queasy look and a squeaky voice, he replied, "Well, that's good." Wanting to quickly change the subject, he asked, "Would you like to sit in the chair, to get you out of that bed for a little while?"

"That sounds good."

He helped me out of bed, and into the big recliner near the window, where the sun could kiss my cheeks. Then…!!

"June, JUNE…"

———————————————————!!!!

———————————————————!!!!

———————————————————!!!!

14

• • • • • •

Brain Dead

Several months into my recovery, I asked what happened during the times I blanked out. Roy, Mindy, and Russell needed to fill in the narrative of my behavior. The first explanation conveyed the removal of the drainage tube.

Roy's explanation of the event:

"Once you made it from the bed to the chair you instantly stopped responding. All you did was stare blankly. I called your name several times, but you wouldn't answer. You appeared to be in some sort of trance! I kept calling your name louder and louder. In a semi-panic, I started yelling at you to answer me! But you wouldn't. That's when I realized you *couldn't*. I was so scared I thought I was going to throw up. For what seemed like a long time I couldn't even think. All you were doing is staring with the tip of your tongue hanging out between your teeth. That alone terrified the crap out of me. Your eyes were glazed over **as though you were brain dead!** Finally, I yell out, "**SOMEONE NEEDS TO HELP US, WE NEED HELP NOW!!**'

"That is when several nurses came rushing in, they tried to get you to respond…but nothing was working! That is when they moved you from the chair, back to the bed and the doctors came rushing in. After examining you, they explained what was happening. 'She is having what is called an absent seizure. She is incapable of responding to anyone. The only way you can help her is by calling in family members or close friends to help coax her out of this state. Is there anyone you can think of that she is close to that can come in to help? Since most of your family members are already deceased, and everyone else lives hours away, my only thought was Mindy. Before Mindy arrived, they had decided to send you back to the Intensive Care Unit. When she came in, the nurses were in the process of transporting you to a gurney so they could bring you to the ICU.

"All of us could see the fear on her face when she first saw you. You in that trance plus the staff surrounding you, she just froze. It was obvious, she had no clue as to what was expect from her. One of the nurses called out, 'June, June, it's your daughter…June, do you hear us? It's your daughter Mindy. Those words transformed her. She pushed her way past everyone. Yet…when she reached you, she gently grabbed your hand and called out, 'Mom, MOM Talk to Me! **MOM!**' After a few more failed attempts of calling you, she began to freak out. That is when she started screaming. **'MOM, Mom pleeeease! PLEASE Talk to ME!**

"Dread completely took over the mood. The doctors and I were now having to calm her down, but she wouldn't listen. She just ignored everyone and everything around her. Then something stopped her, and she started to sing. She was still crying when she sang, but she was calmer. The rest of the room stood back and just watched in amazement. We were all hoping that would work.

'You are my sunshine, my only…♪…♪…♪' "Yet nothing brought you back.

"Then she started panicking again. Everyone in the room felt her pain and we all could see she was refusing to give up. At that point, I felt I had made a big mistake asking her to help. The doctors and I were continuously asking her to calm down, but you know her passion. It didn't help. The doctors were telling her, she absolutely must calm down! They told her, 'This is not helping your mother. You will have to leave and get control of yourself, if you want to help her.'

When our coaxing failed, the doctors tried to physically take her from the room. With all her might, she resisted. The doctors were becoming more and more agitated with her. The whole situation became completely chaotic. I had to get her out of there. So, I gently put my arm around her and finally coaxed her to leave."

Adding to Mindy's trauma; it had only been three years prior when she lost her father to a motorcycle accident. None of the doctors were aware of that fact. All they wanted was for her to leave the room, to get herself under control, and they needed it to happen NOW.

Mindy's explanation:

"When I got the call from Roy and he gave me the news, I flew out of the office. Lena, one of my co-workers, saw me crying in the parking lot. After I explained what had happened, she decided to come to the hospital with me to give support. I flew to the hospital. We were in your room in under 25 minutes."

The medical office where she works is at minimum a 25-minute drive to the hospital under best circumstances, not including finding a spot to park in the parking ramp.

"When I first arrived, the whole room was filled with commotion. I think they were getting you ready to send you up to ICU. Not aware of the full extent of the situation, I stood in a frozen state just watching at first. You were surrounded by the doctors and nurses. Your eyes were just staring at nothing, and your tongue hung out of your mouth like you were already dead! It was the scariest thing I have ever seen! My heart jumped into my throat when I saw you in that state.

Once I realized what was expected of me, I rushed over to you. I felt you would be okay once you saw me. I gently grabbed your hand and called to you. BUT you didn't respond! My mind went into an instant whirlwind of ideas, but I could not bring them out fast enough. I even tried singing to you one of the songs you use to sing when we were little. Yet, no matter what I tried, you weren't responding! All my attempts were failing, causing guilt and torment deep inside of me. I started freezing up, because I could not get you out of that petrified state. I panicked and started screaming because nothing worked. Then, the doctors tried to remove me from the room, but I wasn't about to let that happen. No one, absolutely NO ONE, was taking me away from you! Every part of this situation became out of control.

"I was screaming and crying, **'I DON'T CARE WHAT THE FUCK ALL OF YOU WANT, I AM NOT LEAVING MY MOTHER!'**

"I know the doctors wanted me to leave but that wasn't going to happen. I couldn't leave. To be honest, I really didn't hear a F-ing thing the doctors were saying. They could have told me I just won a 10-million-dollar lottery that day, but I was in such a state of shock I wouldn't have heard them announce it. The only thing I could think about was you in this unspeakable state, gripping me like a vise. I felt I was the **only one** that could bring you back. Then, Roy put his arm around me. At that point I think I was emotionally exhausted, so I gave in and allowed him to convince me to leave. Still, I did not stop watching you. As I was walking out, I noticed your tongue was moving, I pushed every other thought and person, including the doctors, aside and rushed back to sit you up. The tip of your tongue was moving in and out of your mouth as you began heaving. I grabbed a small spit pan as I rushed back, and just as I reached you, you spewed vomit several feet across the room. Not just once, but twice. You had been gagging and choking on your tongue, and no one had really noticed *except* me.

"After the vomiting, it felt safer to leave the room, but I continued to watch you through my tears as I left. I saw your eyes following me, with a slight smile on your lips.

I stopped and called to you, 'I see you. I see you Mom. I see your eyes following me. I love you, Mom!' I finally felt better about leaving, knowing **you weren't brain dead.**"

———————

Mindy still cries to this day (as do I) when recalling that event. Just talking about it makes her re-live it. As she puts it, "I just want to forget every hellish part of that day. It was the most dreadful, vile, devastating, thing I have experienced in my life!"

Roy and Mindy bore the brunt of that traumatic experience, that nightmare was theirs alone. As for me, time had ceased to exist, so I was completely oblivious. Essentially, only my body was there. On the surface, I was <u>brain dead</u>.

After the episode, the doctors led Roy and Mindy to a small conference room, to explain what had caused the seizure. They clung to one another with hugs and tears as the doctors gave details. Dr. M clarified, "Once the tube was removed from June's skull, blood filled the cavity where the tumor had been. That blood built up pressure, pushed on the brain, and caused the seizure she is experiencing. Her mind right now cannot respond to anyone, no matter how hard they try to reach her. So, Mindy, you must calm down and remain calm. You are only making matters worse if you don't."

Dr. M continued, "This is not uncommon. Sometimes it does happen when the drainage tube is removed. We will be sending her back to the Intensive Care Unit for closer observation, but we don't foresee this happening again."

Since I have no memory of this episode, I did not know I had been moved back to ICU. The only thing that contributed to me knowing about the incident, was getting a sponge bath.

As I woke, I felt a warm cloth being applied to my upper body. A friendly faced woman with a sudsy cloth smiled down on me as she continued washing me. My initial reaction to stop her quickly passed because of the total exhaustion from within. In its place, I gave her an approving smile. Her gentle touch, as she cleansed me, made me feel like a baby. Thus, I let the pleasurable feeling linger as the warm sudsy cloth massaged my body. In a weak voice I asked, "Why are you bathing me?"

With a sweet motherly tone, "I am your nurse and we have to make sure you are clean. You already had one UTI. We don't want you to get another one."

Completely oblivious to that fact, I said, "I did?" She just nodded yes.

Under normal circumstances, I would have felt uncomfortable having a stranger bathe me, but feeling weak as a newborn, I enjoyed it. While being bathed, I revealed to her, "I'm not sure why, but I am very worried about vomiting."

With an inquisitive look, the nurse asked, "You are? Why is that?"

"I usually vomit after surgery from the anesthesia, and I didn't this time. I feel like it will hurt a lot more if I were to puke after brain surgery. Just the thought of it has me concerned."

She looked at me with a sweet, understanding smile. "Well if you feel nauseous, we can give you medication to prevent any vomiting."

Smiling back, I said, "That would be great, because I really don't want to throw up."

The only other indications were my extremely dry swollen tongue and degraded speech. My tongue was so engorged and dry it kept sticking to the roof of my mouth. It caused my speech to be worse than it had been when I first came out of surgery. Beyond having trouble getting the correct sounds out of my mouth, I was unable to get food into it. I asked the nurse if there was something that could help.

"You can try some Vaseline. I'll get you some in a moment." When she came back, she handed me a foil package. "Just put a little on your tongue. It should help."

She could clearly see and hear my hesitation, "You mean, I can eat it!?"

"Yes, it's safe. Other patients have found that it to be very helpful."

So, in my mouth it went, and it actually did help. After my sponge bath, and petroleum jelly cocktail, I slept with no memory of that nightmare.

Mindy was so distraught, she felt it necessary to unwind. She and Lena decided it would be a good idea to meet up with their co-workers for dinner. After the other co-workers heard what had happened, they agreed to meet up to help take the heavy burden off her shoulders. As they gathered and cried together, it didn't take long for them to agree. It was time to tell her brother Russell he needed to be here.

Up till now, Mindy had been keeping Russel and Claire in the loop but had left it up to them to decide when wound the best time to make the trip from Virginia. Unbeknownst to any of us they had only hesitated because it meant Russell would have to leave his family once again. Since he received this current update late in the day, he waited until morning to drive the eight hours to New York.

We did not know he had just returned home from two consecutive business trips. Those trips had taken him from his wife and three little girls for a full month. Each trip was two weeks long, one to Colorado, and the other to San Diego. Nevertheless, he and Claire agreed this event had become a game changer for all of us, and it was now necessary for him to be here for me.

But…no one told *me* any part of what had, or was, happening.

15

• • • • • •

Russell's Turn to Experience the Nightmare

I was just waking up with the vision of Russell looking down at me. It had me thinking how much I wished he was with me. But…I was the one who told him it wasn't necessary to come while I was in the hospital. So, I needed to be understanding. Yet, as I focused deeper, and opened my eyes wider, I realized it really was him in the flesh. My heart swelled and I almost cried I felt so happy. It was such a wonderful surprise! Yet, a small touch of sadness came over me. *I hoped my surgery hadn't pushed him to choose between me and his family. But, either way, I love having him by my side, and I was going to enjoy every minute with him.*

Roy stepped out of the room to grab some coffee, which gave us some private time together. His exit allowed my focus to be on Russell and enjoy his company. I felt complete with both of my children and Roy watching over me. I knew they all had their own anxieties, so I felt compelled to show everyone how far I had come with my recovery. As "the Mom", it was my obligation to set a good example by being strong and demonstrating how to handle life's challenges. For me, everything was great. I had no memory of the last few days; all I saw was my family showing their loving support while I started my recovery.

Everything was fine until I realized I needed to use the restroom. That had me feeling a little frustrated because of that *sucky bed alarm!* But

Russell came to my rescue and without me even asking, he turned it off. *Yay, someone helped me escape from the bed shackles! At least that was the way I felt at the time.* That alone put a big smile on my face. I felt pleased my walking had improved so Russell didn't have to view me walking with weak bowlegs.

Nonetheless, everything started to go downhill from there. After opening the restroom door, I turned back with a scrunched up look on my face. The toilet still had my roommate's plastic "hat" in the bowl, and it was full. Not wanting to take any chances with my health, I decided it would be best to wait until that collection hat was removed by the nurse.

Russell asked inquisitively, "Mom, are you okay?"

"Yes and no, I don't want to use this room because the toilet needs to be cleaned."

"Oh, okay, that's understandable. I'll get a nurse or housekeeping to come in." As he searched for someone, I went back to bed. They must have been busy, because after several minutes, no one came in. While waiting, good friends of the family, Zoila and Harold, came for a morning visit. Surprised and pleased I said, "What a nice surprise. It is so good to see you guys. Had I known you were coming in I would have at least combed my hair."

Hairstyle after surgery (2)

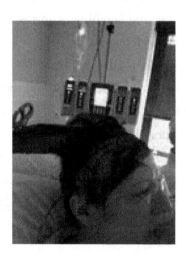

Zoila said, "You look fine, don't you worry." She's always kind like that, but if anyone could have seen my hair and swollen face, they might be laughing too. Because of the 56 stitches on my skull, I could only use dry shampoo, and that left my hair looking more like the down of a baby bird (a very large bird) that had recently hatched. So, we all had a good laugh.

Although the visit was a pleasant distraction, my bladder was reaching capacity. That was when I suggested we take a walk to find a different restroom. I had been told it was good for me to walk. Hence, we could accomplish two important tasks at the same time. There were three other adults with me. Russell had stopped at the front desk and informed the nurse of our trip and since they did not try to stop us, we thought it was okay. We all felt full of confidence, knowing we could handle this. What could possibly go wrong? Everything was fine as we walked, laughed, and searched not knowing an unpredictable nightmare was following us. We went around the corner and down another hall, before we finally found another restroom.

Zoila asked, "Do you need me to come in with you? Do you need any help?"

"Thank you, but no. I'm fine." I truly thought I was, but just in case I left the door unlocked.

Plus, my shyness prevented me from wanting her in the room with me. I could hear them talking and laughing from the other side of the door. It had me feeling uncomfortable, because I realized they could hear me… and my bodily noises. I felt embarrassed. Therefore, I took care of business and tried my best to do it quietly. Every now and then, Zoila would shout out, "How are you doing? Is everything okay?"

"Yes, things are fine," I semi-lied. My digestive system was not functioning well, but I needed to resolve the discomfort. I was extra careful because I knew that too much strain could cause harm even under the best circumstances. A few minutes later, with a little more concern in her voice, "June, are you still okay? I'm getting a little worried out here."

Trying not to alarm them, I lied again, "No need to worry, I am fine. I'll be out in a moment after I wash." Upon standing, I started to feel a little fuzzy. I took some deep breaths and tried to convince myself I was fine. While washing my hands, things started to feel better, especially as I splashed my face with cold water. At the same time, things began taking a drastic turn for the worse. I felt unsafe, I knew I better get out of that room fast! So, I rushed to get out the door.

I opened the door…looked up, and I was in a dark room with a woman with long black hair leaning down looking back at me. Freakishly disoriented I realized I was in bed, and everyone else was gone! Totally mystified I asked in a demanding voice, "Where is my son?" (at the same time *Wondering where I was and why I was in bed)* "And where are Harold and Zoila?"

With a kind but remorseful look on her face she apologized. She leaned in a little closer to make certain I could hear her, or perhaps to check my eyes. "I'm the hospital's Chief Administrator. Can you tell me what happened? Are you okay?"

Extremely bewildered…I was wondering if all that had just taken place had been a dream, and if not, where was everyone? Why am I back in bed? While trying to process what was real, I finally replied, "What do you mean? We went for a walk to use a different restroom because this one was dirty."

"We are all so sorry this entire incident happened to you. Are you okay now? Can you tell us how you are feeling now? Does your head hurt? Did you hit your head?"

I looked at her, like she had two heads. "I don't know what you are talking about."

Then I noticed an elderly woman, with a kind face, smiling at me from across the room. With her bright red hair, that lay snug to her head she could not be missed even though she is very petite. She was the woman that had been cleaning my room.

"Again, we are all so very sorry. None of this should have occurred. You probably strained too much and that is what caused the episode."

With an exasperated heavy breath, I asked… "What episode? What, are you talking about?"

"You had a vasovagal episode."

"What is a vaso…or whatever-you-just-said, episode?"

As she explained, I listened with a stunned look, "A vasovagal is a form of fainting. It can be caused by straining or by stomach cramps. None of this is your fault. I am just glad you are okay."

"Okay…but I don't remember a thing, except walking to the bathroom and using the facility. I remember getting a little dizzy, but that is all."

"You probably just strained a little too hard. Sometimes that can bring the episodes on. Again, none of this should have taken place, and we will be sure it doesn't happen again. You can call me if you need anything… anything at all."

She left and a nurse came in to take my vital signs. While we were talking, she casually mentioned, "That was how Elvis Presley died."

In total disbelief and wondering why she said that, I replied, "You're kidding, right?"

"No, it's true."

With a stunned exasperated tone "Oh, swell!" was all I could say.

Although it was true Elvis did die in the bathroom, he really died of a drug overdose, unlike me who just had a bowel movement. Ugh!

I do not remember what followed that conversation. But I do remember being very sad, because I did not get to see any of my family or friends until the next day. Once again…more lost time!

It took quite a lot of practice before I could even say the word "vasovagal" correctly. I kept asking how to pronounce it. Now, I not only know how to pronounce it, but I know how to prevent it from happening. Shortly after, the doctors came in to check on me. "Well how are you feeling now? How is your head?"

Shaking my head and snickering, I said, "My head is fine, but I am not sure which part of my body has more control: my brain or my bowels."

After some laughter, the doctor agreed. "Yes, I have been in that situation myself, and I believe the bowels win. We are going to prescribe something to help move things along. Please let us know if we can help you in any other way."

Although it truly was not funny, and it could have been so much worse, I had to laugh because I needed to feel better. The way I looked at it, if you are not laughing, you are probably going to cry. I'd rather laugh and try to enjoy life's adventures, including my bodily mishaps.

On the other hand, Roy was utterly furious!! He was upset and blaming everyone for allowing this to happen. He was totally frustrated, exhausted, and pissed off at everyone for all the drama the family had gone through. The never-ending series of nightmares had him on his last nerve and completely drained.

Russell's explanation from his perspective:
What he went through when I came out of the restroom:

"You grabbed my hand as you walked out of the room and without so much as a blink of your eyes, you instantly became dead weight. Immediately, I went into shock as time seemed to slow down. You became a rag doll that was now slipping straight through my fingers. I watched the nightmare unfolding in a very long-drawn-out moment. I was desperately trying to find something to take a hold of on you to prevent you, from falling, but you were in a fluid state. At least that is what it seemed like, because there was absolutely nothing to grab! At that very instant…I visualized your head slamming onto the floor! That is when my caretaker reflex kicked in. Just in time, I was able to catch your head in my hands before it hit the floor. I can still picture and feel that scene, over and over again. It is burned into my memory. Guilt and shock filled my whole being, seeing you stretched out on the floor. I looked around for assistance and saw that Harold and Zoila were also in the pursuit of help. Then I saw Roy walking down the hall. Knowing he probably saw the whole thing unfolding before his eyes had me feeling even worse. He rushed to your side, yelling for help. By that time, the nurses and doctors were already rushing down the hallway."

That ordeal was very harsh on everyone involved. We were all distressed. My distress was caused from not knowing. It had been my body lying there on the floor, but my mind was nowhere to be found. I did not remember the fall or the slam to my body.

I now understand how some people on drugs have no recollection of their own actions, or the activities around them. Perhaps, needless to say, it was my children, Roy, and close friends, who were going through hell and back several times over. I have only partial memories of any of the last two episodes, I was only aware of the before-and-after shocks. I did not feel pain or discomfort. I cannot imagine how I would have reacted if I had been the one watching my mom have an absent seizure, impelled vomit across the room, or had her collapse in my arms, unable to prevent the fall! But my family can. They had to hold it all together. They had to assist me to obtain help, then carry on. They were my inspiration, even though I was supposed to be theirs.

16

·•·•••·•·

I Tried to be Strong

Without having the knowledge of the absent seizure, I carried on like I was totally improving. However, my mind and especially my speech were more depleted, which was evident by my actions. My language skills brought me the most frustration, but I dealt with it through laughter. I could not find the correct words to even start sentences. Sometimes I couldn't connect single words correctly in my own thoughts. No matter how much I slowed down to concentrate on each word, they still came out a jumbled mess. I simply could not connect my thoughts properly. Like a drunken college student, I was laughing my way through a new self-taught foreign language. Sometimes it seemed as though, I could only find some of the words in my mind as others within the same sentence eluded me totally. I wanted to tell everyone I was doing well, instead it came out all jubbled; "I can, well I could, I'm great! I don't feel only, I mean not much at all." I was trying to tell them, "I can't get my words to connect correctly." My brain wasn't healed enough yet to bring the thoughts to my tongue. It was like what happens to a stroke victim. Everyone understood and would say, "You sound great, don't worry."

Deep inside I knew they were just being kind and for the moment that was fine with me, because I was so happy to be alive. I knew what I meant most of the time. But as it continued to fail me, I started to get anxious. There were times, the lack of correct synapses in my brain would become frustrating and very odd. I felt like a clown, laughing on the outside yet concerned on the inside that my language and cognitive skills might never improve completely.

When I tried demonstrating my improvements and strength, by being happy to be alive, my attempts backfired. Being playful and laughing after almost every joke, I remember saying, "You're batting a thousand with that one. Haa haa haa." (The painful truth was…not everything said had been a joke, nor was it funny.) My family was now giving me sympathetic smiles and wondering if I was going to "La la land" perhaps permanently. We were all traveling down this steep unknown path and confusion harassed us with every step.

Along with the intent to be strong, my desire to write a book about my experience never stopped. It was an imbedded motivation throughout all the turmoil. In spite of this, my intended writing frightened my family. It bothered my son, the most. What was meant to help, brought apprehension. This became evident when I saw him reading my notations and a few minutes later I overheard him on a phone conversation with his wife, Claire. He had my notes in his hand and he was sharing them with her. I smiled and told him why I had been writing things down. I tried to explain, I am writing to chart my improvements plus to write a book to share my experience. "I am hoping, by recording what is occurring, I might eventually see improvements. That, in turn, might keep me motivated and strong."

With a look of concerned sadness, he said, "Yeah, I see."

Although I wasn't certain why he had concerns, I suspected he knew something about them that I didn't. A few weeks into recovery, when I re-read what I had written, I discovered why Russell had apprehensions when he read my comments. My writing was like that of song writers that were high on drugs. Both they and I thought our initial drafts were at least good. But, to the casual reader, they were outlandish!

The following are some of my notes I wrote while in the hospital:

"Starting two memory by remembering to in I stay healthier."

"Still forgetting which words to chose."

"Still having trouble Still having trouble remembering."

"Brough up two great adults."

"Blubbling threw the my front teeth."

"Different I see shadows, jointing sentences /thoughts it is harder to join/thoughts connecting sentences more different sometimes."

Those were word for word, spelled exactly that way. When I wrote those comments, I was incapable of finding correct words in my mind, no matter how hard I tried. Spelling? Forget it! it felt like I needed to learn to talk all over again let alone spell the word correctly. Instead of my family seeing me as capable, my writing caused them more distress. I had not given much thought ahead of time, how it would alarm my family, but it had me rethinking after seeing my son's reaction.

Life had introduced another dimension to all of us and none of us knew if my stay was permanent. The whole situation was upsetting my family more each day. It utterly terrified me! All I could do was hold onto hope that I would improve as I moved forward. Despite that, none of us were aware how long it would take, or if all of us would feel pleased with the final outcome. Since I continued to be out of touch with reality, my children no longer thought of me as strong, they thought of me as weak and mentally inadequate.

17

· · · • · · ·

The "Fight" to Go Home

I felt a strong pull to be back home as I laid awake thinking about much needed sleep. My swollen tongue, along with no longer being able to taste, kept me from eating, plus my new roommate had the TV on 24/7. The light was more bothersome than the sound, because at night it would shine like a full moon in the room. Even when silence finally fell at night, the nurse's call bell would ring out periodically. My understanding for the other patients' needs was wearing thin. It all added to my angst. Add to the facts that I wasn't able to take a relaxing shower, not to mention use the bathroom in private and being tethered to that damned bed, had me irritated and longing for home. All of the family was on a sharply fringed cliff, with our emotions teetering on the edge. The irritations grew one by one and hounded all of us. Everyone's blood pressure was off the charts as we tried to maneuver around this medical/emotional mine field. Even though I was oblivious to some events, especially when my body failed me, there were plenty of times I knew exactly what was occurring. There were even times when bickering was the only way to get through some of this stressful nightmare! And arguing, especially shortly after brain surgery, is not what one should be doing.

Another day, another attempt to start the day with a desire to improve and prove I could do anything I set my mind to, including recover from brain surgery. In an arrogant, selfish mood,

I was determined to push myself harder. Instead of being smart and taking this one step at a time, I insisted I had recovered more than I actually had. My ignorance was fooling only myself, but the pressure cooker within me was ready to spill over. I had enough of this situation and at that point I simply didn't give a rat's ass… I wanted out of the hospital.

Dr. H., the neurosurgeon, visited me on Thursday June 28th, in a reserved but positive mood. "Everything appears to be coming along very well. All your tests and scans show you are improving. It also shows the swelling of the brain has subsided. I think we can talk about you going home soon, perhaps Monday."

Without even thinking about it, I seized the opportunity. With a smile on my face and arrogance in my voice, I disagreed, "No, I am going home tomorrow!"

His demeanor quickly changed to astonishment, "Well, I don't know about that. We will have to see."

Shaking my head yes, I insisted and repeated, "I am going home tomorrow."

Roy joined in, "June, you need to listen to the doctor, and if he says you can go home on Monday, we should listen to him."

My resolve was stronger than before, "Nooo! I am going home tomorrow. I feel great, I don't have any pain, and I don't want to be tethered to this bed any longer. I will be better off at home. My voice raised a tad louder, "I **need** to go home."

Trying to help, Russell spoke up, "Mom, Roy is right this time. You need to listen to your doctor's advice."

"I don't care who thinks what I should do. All of you do not understand how I feel." And all of us, including me, did not know the whole picture. Wanting to keep the family peace, I not only needed to go home, I believed that I absolutely HAD to. I could not tell anyone why, but I needed to stop all the fighting and anguish. Although in different ways, we were all going through some very anxious times. So, I told them it was because I hated being strapped to the bed (which was true) but it wasn't the whole story. I spouted out a directive, "I want to go home, and whether any of you say so or not, I am going home tomorrow!"

The mood in the room quickly changed to frustration and a fight of wills. The doctor was not about to clash with me, so all he said was, "Let me see what I can do." Then he left.

Roy was beside himself and he also left. Russell stayed, trying to reason with me. But I was not about to give in. "Mom, I remember when grandma was in the hospital, and you had to tell her she needed to listen to the doctors. Now you are doing the exact same thing she used to do."

I needed to give him a reason he would believe, yet not tell him the full truth, because it would cause more grief. Deep within, my love for my family, was fueling me to end this nightmare. My affliction was the cause and I had to be the solution. Not knowing how to say that without causing more pain I gave an excuse that I thought they would accept. "You don't understand how hard it is to be a woman who needs to be independent. And now I am pushed so far down I can't even get up to go pee by myself. I need to stop depending on all of this help to get my true recovery started."

With tears in my eyes, partially because I needed his understanding, and partially because I felt so bad about the real reasons, I continued my explanation. Using a more persuasive voice, "I am a very independent woman, and now I'm tethered to this bed like a child. I must call for a nurse just to walk five feet to the restroom. I can't take this. I need to go home!" With a composed tone, "I will be okay. Please try to understand, I need to be home."

What I knew was I needed to get on with my recovery and stop the in-house fighting and anguish. In my eyes, the only way to do that was to leave the hospital. The doctor came back later that day to let me know: I could indeed go home. It was not going to be tomorrow, but I could leave on Saturday, the following day. I felt, at least it was a few less days in the hospital. One of the conditions for my discharge was to pass the test given by the physical therapists to prove I was physically able enough to leave.

18

• • • • • •

Lack of Physical Coordination

The therapist came in that following morning, Friday, June 29th. She was a pleasant young lady. "Hello, my name is Jennifer. I am assigned to your case. I am here to see what you are capable of doing. Would you please walk to the bathroom door for me?"

As she observed my walk, I straightened my back and proudly walked to the door for her. I had a lot of practice doing that, so I was totally confident I would pass that task. In fact, that could be done rather easily. She smiled and said, "Okay that was good."

Feeling proud that I showed her how well I was doing, I was ready for the next request.

Continuing her assessment, she instructed, "Now try walking with one foot in front of the other."

I called out, "Whoa, what the heck?" As I weaved and wobbled, feeling drunk and failing what felt like a sobriety test. "I thought that was going to be a lot easier." That invisible slap on the back of my head, brought me to the harsh reality of my condition. She simply smiled back at me. Next, at a very fast pace like an auctioneer, or at least that is what it sounded like to me, she said, "Okay, now try touching your nose with your right hand, then bring your left hand up, and place that on top of your right hand, while your right hand is still on your nose."

The pressure was on and I choked! That request left me feeling like I had just been zapped with a taser. Trying to figure out what she just said, let alone doing it, was not happening. I looked at her with confusion and disbelief. *Was she mocking me?* Not only did the directions confuse me, but she was totally aware I would not be able to do it. She proved to me I was not as strong mentally or physically as I thought or professed to be. Deep inside, I felt she was showing me things were not the same as they had been before surgery. And, I better get used to taking things slower.

That one command humbled me back to the real world. It was a wakeup call, and caused me to realize I had a lot to learn about life after brain surgery. I still sensed I could overcome the challenges ahead but, I had to admit, it stopped me from being so damned smug! In fact, I began to intensely question whether it was still a good idea to leave the hospital. But, with all the confusion and unrest, my whole being knew I had made the right choice.

Life-threatening situations often take on a full life of their own. They try to steal your spirit and soul. If you let them, it will definitely win! Without much effort, it will turn your whole life upside down and inside out. It shows you; you are no longer the person you were prior to the misfortune. For example, every time I look at my face, scratch my rutted skull, try to smell or taste something, I realize I am changed physically and psychologically. But, I am still the strong woman I was before I had the surgery. In fact, I am stronger and more determined, and even though I FAILED most of those physical tests, Jennifer still gave me the OK to leave. I think even she saw my strength.

19

•••••••

The Adventure of Recovery

During the first few days after my return to home, I noticed the days passed slowly. The days, almost seemed to be watching over me, not knowing what to do to keep me occupied or motivated. I think it was due to being scared and alone for part of that time. But that started to change as I noticed the warmth and softness of mother nature beckoning me to cheer up. Once I realized that each day had precious little treasures, without seizures or frightening hallucinations, I was happier. The fun days of recovery began and brought all the great pleasures I was able to share with others.

So much of what had transpired was painfully agonizing. Yet some of it, believe it or not, was truly remarkable and even fun. All I truly knew at that time was…I had something to prove. I had to prove I could recover and get my life back. I could enjoy life again, but perhaps in a different way.

Thinking back to when recovery first started, I could not even stand up straight, nor walk correctly, because my brain was not cooperating. Even eating was a chore. My tongue and face became so swollen that I literally had to push food in through a little opening in my mouth, because I couldn't open it wide enough. Talking, walking, even thinking, all added to the gloom. There was the encounter with death staring me in the face, as I felt "**it**" was going to win! It was an eerie, cowardly phantom that seemed to reach out from behind, trying to grab me at the point when I felt broken and defeated. I'll probably never forget that moment the phantom reached for me!

It was late at night, and all was quiet in my dimly lit room. I was headed to the restroom with help from a nurse. I can even remember what I was thinking at that instant. I was wondering if my legs were going to remain bowed forever. At that precise moment, I became weaker as I felt its dark presence hovering over me. I sensed it wanted to take my soul. My whole body felt crippled with fear! I didn't want to do anything except stand very still, trying to be invisible, hoping it would not find me. All I could do was pray for strength. It was a sense of anger that ignited a fire within my soul and internally I yelled out! *I'm not ready to die yet!* It was so loud I thought for sure the nurse heard it. I told "It", *God is on my side, you need to leave. I'm too young to die! You can take me when I am in my eighties or nineties but NOT NOW!* That event frightened me so much, that recalling it still summons fear in me.

As for the absent seizure and blackouts I suffer from while in the hospital and at home, I compare them to death. One minute I would be fully awake and aware, and the next moment I was completely oblivious to <u>everything</u> including pain. I just "stopped". And I have wondered...*If that is what **death** will be like?* That alone is a particularly uncomfortable feeling and unpleasant in a weird way. It is extremely hard to put these feelings into words. I am not devastated by it, but...there is a fundamental loss when you just **stop <u>existing</u>**. I feel a small part of ME was taken with each episode. **Regardless of how small,** those experiences were, they stole a part of me when they occurred. The one thing these events gave me in return, was a continuous craving for life and recovery. Due to that burning desire, I was more motivated to find the finish line before going through the, necessary, steps. Pushing myself intensely required me to dig deep, to prohibit any delusional fears from sabotaging my goal. I could not listen to the voice within that crept up and said, *You just had brain surgery, you must slow down. You're weak and fragile. You should not be pushing yourself so hard.* However, I did allow that voice to lead me to break down my recovery into little victories, in order to succeed. It was vital to think of each little success as a semi-major triumph, small stages, yet large enough for me to feel that I was succeeding. I kept repeating to myself daily, *one step at a time…one step at a time. Then the steps can lead to yards, and once again I will be able to relax, and enjoy life to its fullest.*

When I first came home, the stairs scared me the most. I literally did not even want to look at them. There was no way I was going to attempt to climb them. So, I slept downstairs the first few days. As I looked at the steps, I was worried I was going to fall all the way down them. My first few ventures at climbing them, I held onto the rail for dear life. I pulled myself up, one hand over the other as though climbing a steep slope with a rope. Going down, I leaned into the rail with my back and hands. I gripped the rail as though it was a lifeline, slowly taking one step at a time as I descended. It paid off. In less than two weeks, I was walking up and down the stairs with little or no problem.

As fate would have it, we were very fortunate that Mindy and Michael had moved in with us, especially since I was on 24/7 watch the first month that I was home. My brother Lou also came to my rescue and stayed with me a few hours a day. Two to three times a week a visiting nurse would come in to check on my progress. It wasn't always the same nurse, but it did not matter they were all very kind to me. They would all tell me, "You should take it easy and be careful." But I had something to prove, so I pushed on without taking their advice. I not only had to prove it to the world, I had to prove it to myself. Death had already grabbed a few pieces of me; I was not going to weaken and let it take more. I could do all that I used to do again. And I desperately wanted to get back to work, especially now that I had achieved my degree, and Roy was beyond ready to retire.

Each night I would go to bed with a goal in mind for the next day. I even decided how I was going to dress to achieve that goal. One beautiful summer morning I dressed, knowing I was going to have a visiting nurse come to our home. I was all ready to show her my progress and that everything was going very well. When she was leaving, I decided to walk her out and grab the mail. Since our mailbox is across the street, I think the nurse decided to wait in her car while I retrieved it. I was not thinking about what Michael had just told me a few days prior: "Nana, be careful when you get the mail, there is a bee's nest in there."

However, my memory kicked into high gear as I reached into the box and the bees came out in full stinging fashion. Perhaps, needless to say, they did not appreciate being disturbed. Out they came as I ran in the opposite direction. Nonetheless, what most people take for granted, like running away from bees, was not an easy option for me so soon after brain surgery. I wavered and weaved like a piece of ribbon candy, all the while thinking I would be kissing the pavement at any moment! To my pleasant surprise, I was able to move away from the bees before they stung me for a third time. Yes, I got stung. Great progress is relative…the good news is; I DID NOT FALL ON THE ROAD!

The next time I had the pleasure of engaging my running ability was a few weeks later. My son and his beautiful family came to visit and decided to camp in our backyard. It was such an awesome way to visit! Our backyard is a very inviting site for camping. Our Koi pond and the songs from the bullfrogs just beg for creatures of all persuasion to visit. The night before they arrived, Michael and I shared a great Nana and grandson moment when we slept under the stars in my tent. We had a great time watching funny videos on my iPhone before the warm summer breeze soothed us both to sleep. It was a good thing we did, because the next night there was rain with thunder and lightning. There was no way I was sleeping outside in a tent under those weather conditions, although Russell, Claire, and the girls bravely slept outside. Before the rain came, the sense of adventure grew as Roy's daughter, Michele, and his grandson, Aiden, joined us for an outdoor movie and campfire.

On Sunday, the weather had improved. <u>Improved</u>, well…when it comes to weather, is also a relative word. The rain had passed but the wind decided to stick around and escalate. It not only picked up speed, it decided our tent would make a good kite, especially since there were no strings attached. I realized it was flying in the wind when I saw my son running after it as it blew across the road into the neighbor's yard. Once more I had to put my running shoes on to help grab it.

Even though, running <u>is not</u> a safe thing for post-brain surgery patients, it felt wonderful to be able to flex my muscles and feel like a kid. Plus, someone needed to help Russell retrieve that tent. It turned out to be great fun! Running…well…Russell was running while I weaved back and forth like a drunk. It was a good thing I was there to help because, as we grabbed it, the tent was grabbing us, attempting to take us parasailing. It was very hard to grab, scary, and funny all in one shot.

It made for a funny adventure story. The only bad part was, we missed an opportunity to get it all on film and enter the video in the TV show "Funniest Home Videos". I would have loved to see us on film, and I bet we would have won the grand prize!

20

······

A New "Me"

Some days, my body was just an entity traveling on its own without help from my thought processes. I was constantly needing to validate each detail of my thoughts and memories because "I" no longer trusted my own brain or sense of self. A lot of the details of my ordeal still remains a mystery, as though they are meant to be kept secret. Sometimes I think this is a good thing because now that more of the memories are surfacing, and I am made more aware, my fears have grown ten times more intense. Post trauma stress is mine to bear now. When I get even a little extra warm or see a shadow, I quickly go on guard. It has me wondering if something bad is about to happen.

It is true, life dealt me a difficult hand and the insecurities it brought had become my evil enemy! The guts and resolve to move forward did not always show themselves to me. There were plenty of times I did not even want to face reality. The only way I knew how to do that, was to fake it. The workaround was to maneuver with laughter…and many times all that came out were tears.

With all the abruptness and changes, like any amputation of the body, a different person is created. Although brain surgery is not as physically visible as other amputations, it is still an amputation of sorts, with deformities, especially of the face and skull. Without much effort, my recovery unquestionably stole a large chunk of my confidence, which in my case plummeted by at least forty percent.

Sometimes I felt downright ugly, especially with the visible facial and skull deformities, and the obvious brain and body malfunctions. My motor skills became less than graceful, words came out any way they fancied, my cooking went from average to awful, including the burning of food, because I could no longer smell anything. Not surprisingly, some friends and family members started to treat me differently. Although I knew they all meant well, it led me to think differently about myself. So, I fought against the extra help they offered. I needed to feel I could still do all that I had before, even if I was not capable of it yet.

Then I remembered the "portal" I had seen in the recovery room. It had me wondering. Had that been there to show me the path I was required to travel for recovery? Perhaps it was showing me, even though the path might be dark and sometimes murky (like the unknown usually is) it could be trusted, because the outer perimeter was lit by the glow from my faith. I just needed to trust that I would be guided and moved away from any more extreme occurrences...the worst was over, and I could, and should, move forward uninhibited now. Hence, I had to grab control and walk through that darkness to reach my goals and trust again.

So, one step at a time, I took back my confidence. In the first few weeks after leaving the hospital I was even afraid to go outside in the sunshine, because of the steroid medication. I also still had a fear of blacking out while home alone. Yet, it was imperative to find something to improve my sense of well-being. Therefore, I slowly pushed our sliding glass door open and walked onto our deck. It felt wonderful as the warmth caressed my face and limbs. Despite the fact I was still worried, each time I went out for a longer time period. Sometimes I would sit under an umbrella on our deck and just watch the fish swim in our Koi pond. Some days, I would just watch the whole day go by, while I enjoyed the beautiful sounds of Mother Nature.

All of that led me to the desire to take a walk. So, I dressed in my long exercise outfit to protect my skin from the sun, fetched my backpack, packed it with a bottle of water, a small snack, and my cellphone. Then, I grabbed an umbrella to use for a cane and more protection from the sun, and last, but certainly not least, I coaxed Michael to come with me. As we walked, we enjoyed each other's company and got our exercise. I worked my way up to a two-mile walk. It really helped me to feel so much happier and healthier as I continued to reach my little goals. Each day I improved more and more; and the unforeseen gain was, I began to lose weight. I lost 20 pounds just walking a few days a week.

The in-home care provider noticed that, although I was physically getting better, emotionally I was still drained. She recommended that I get out even more and perhaps make an appointment for my hair. Sadly, I replied, "But not all hair stylists can work on women with such a large gap of missing hair, let alone someone who has such a large scar on their scalp."

"That may be true, but I happen to know of a very good stylist who can. Her name is Daisy. I'll get the phone number so you can call her. Just make the call and see what she says. I am certain she will be able to help you."

21

......

New Hairstyle Brings Emotional Wellness

Daisy's help was truly wonderful. Who knew a hairstylist could help so much? Certainly not me. There I was, receiving the all essential emotional push that I needed. She gave me such an emotional transformation, I felt the need to dedicate a chapter to her. She is a wonderful lady and her salon is very relaxing. She makes you feel like you are visiting with family and that you matter. I know I am not the only one she has helped in that way.

I will never forget my first appointment with her. Daisy made me feel like she wanted to know me from the inside. She cares about her client's psyche. Daisy knows the value of helping the "whole" person, body and soul. She also teaches that value to the other beauticians in her shop.

When I arrived, I looked like a blow-up doll that was over inflated with a bad haircut. And I truly did not feel good about being in public. The other beauticians were all involved with their own clients when I entered. Yet, even after their clients were gone, they stayed and watched Daisy work her magic on me that night. It made me feel extra special as they also wanted to watch her (as I call it), perform.

Daisy had me feeling so beautiful by the end of the appointment I felt whole once again. It made me realize how much my confidence had collapsed. It wasn't until she had finished and whirled the chair around for me to see, that I realized a grand transformation had taken place. My whole being came rushing back to me at that moment. The feeling was so grand, I can still feel that sensation today as I write the words. It makes me wish I was a better writer so I could articulate that feeling more skillfully. I went into an emotional shock when I first saw myself in the mirror. It was like all the past bad experiences had never happened. For what seemed like a long drawn out moment, even **I forgot** I **was recovering** from brain surgery. That split-second of realizing I had forgotten caused my emotions to rush forward flooding my tear ducts. My tears were expressing deep feelings of joy. The whole room paused as they also felt my emotions when my tears fell. It was the most therapeutic session I have ever had the pleasure of experiencing. She made me feel real again. It was truly a majestic feeling.

When I went out to show Roy, I danced around on the sidewalk with joy before getting into the car. Michael told me how nice it looked, and I saw tears flow from Roy's eyes because he saw how happy it made me feel. I felt a huge weight lift from me as we drove home. That appointment was an enormous part of my recovery because it helped to bring me back to my norm.

"Thank you again, Daisy!"

22

•••••••

I Never Gave Up

Six months later I was out Christmas shopping and enjoying life again. I bumped into old friends and was able to catch up on what I had missed. I was so glad they saw me in an advanced convalescent state, because they could spread the word that I was doing well and looked better than the last time they had seen me. I can now look at myself in the mirror and see a happier, much healthier me. I see a reflection that does not scare or shock me. I still see the wrinkles and some gray hair, but those are good things.

Some days, even eight months later, I still sit and cry when the insecurities sneak in and cause small miseries. I still do not have a job, I still spill things, burn myself, forget easily, get a little depressed, and feel deformed. But I fight it. I don't give up. I keep moving forward. I know I am so much better than I was even two months previous. I continue to see more progress each week. Although the steps I take are the same ones, I now see new lessons learned and a clearer view of the path. Just like with every other life experience, all those lessons will lead me to the correct path and a stronger soul.

In all, it has taken me seven plus years of **editing** to obtain the correct wording and formulating for my sentences to make this memoir pleasurable to read. Yet I have never given up on my book or my recovery.

Live your own life, find your lessons, fight for your goals, and **never** give up on your dreams. Pass on what you have learned to the next generation. They may not want to hear it, but then again, it just might help them someday.

It is how we handle struggles that give us our mark in life and define who we are or will become. I did not want to just sit back and let my larger-than-life scar take me down. That is why I had to find a way to turn this to something positive. It led me to write this memoir and share that knowledge.

I know now this is a part of my true destiny, my personal serendipity. I feel that I was meant to tell this story. It is, my special place in life, and I am exactly where I am meant to be. I am a storyteller, a teacher at heart. I like who I am and all the progress I have made.

ACKNOWLEDGEMENTS
AND GRATITUDE

I have so many people to thank for my recovery and for this memoir. I give thanks to my family for holding me up and being by my side when I was out of touch with reality and the world as we know it. I also want to thank them for filling in the blanks and giving me their opinions. A special thank you and recognition goes to my husband for his understanding and patience as I wrote and read this memoir to him repeatedly while editing. I need to acknowledge and thank my new friend Marie B. for the help she gave me with editing and so much more.

This experience truly terrified me! Nevertheless, it also taught me a lot about life, love, faith, and myself. With that in mind, it also taught me to never give up and fight for what is important.

APPENDIX A--PICTURES

Before, during, and After Pictures:

Hairstyle Before surgery (1)

#1. Just before surgery with my tribal head-dress. Happy to be getting the tumor OUT of me. An ultimate "lala land" photo

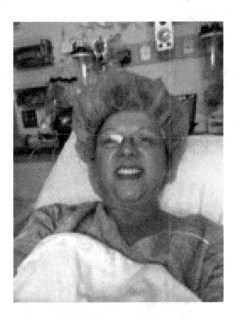

#2. One day after surgery, swollen with new hair style I call the "skater babe look." AKA "Over-inflated-blow-up-doll with a bad haircut and glasses."

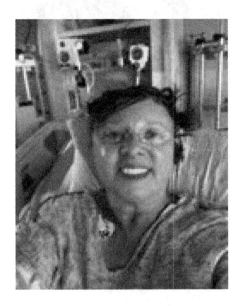

#3. Surgical scar where they cut and drilled along with the drainage tube

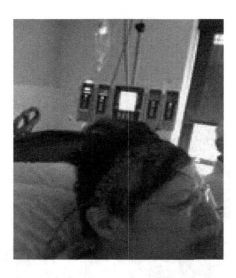

#4. I was "Out on the Town" with my RED socks! Patients at risk of falling had to wear them. I appear shorter due to the problem with my gait (weak & bow-legged) but still smiling

#5. After the appointment with Daisy

WORKS CITED

https://www.epilepsy.com/learn/about-epilepsy-basics/what-happens-during-seizure 9/14/2019 9:50 AM

http://wiki.answers.com/frontal+to+the+lobes+of+the+b 9/5/2012 8:10 PM

The **frontal lobe** controls: Drive; Mood; Memory; Attention; Initiation; Language; Judgment; Spontaneity; Motor function; Impulse control; Problem solving; Social behavior; Feeling of empathy and sympathy; Mental planning and execution.

What happens if your **Frontal Lobe** in the **brain** is **damaged**?

Printed in the United States
By Bookmasters